Zermatt
Hiking Adventures
2024

Exploring the Swiss Alps

Kieran Tucker

Copyright © 2024, Kieran Tucker.

All rights reserved.

No part of this publication may be reproduced, distributed, or transmitted in any form or by any means, including photocopying, recording, or other electronic or mechanical methods, without the prior written permission of the publisher, except in the case of brief quotations embodied in critical reviews and certain other noncommercial uses permitted by copyright law.

Table of Contents

About This Guide..**8**

Introduction to Zermatt..**9**

    Welcome to Zermatt..9

    A Brief History of Zermatt...9

    Zermatt in 2024: What's New?..10

Geography and Climate of Zermatt...**13**

    Geography...13

    Climate..14

    Impact on Hiking..15

Planning Your Zermatt Hiking Adventure..**17**

    Research and Preparation..17

    Planning Your Itinerary...17

    Final Preparations...18

Preparing For Your Zermatt Hiking Adventure..................................**19**

    Essential Gear and Equipment..19

    Safety Tips and Guidelines...20

    Weather Considerations..22

    Health and Fitness Preparations..23

Getting to Zermatt..**25**

Travel Options to Zermatt..25

Transportation in Zermatt..26

Accommodation Options..27

Top Hiking Trails in Zermatt...33

Gornergrat: A Panoramic Adventure..33

The Matterhorn Trail: Iconic Views..35

Five Lakes Walk: Scenic Beauty..38

Hike to Zmutt: Historic and Picturesque...41

Edelweissweg: Flower-filled Paths...44

Glacier Trail: Ice and Adventure..46

Family Friendly Hikes in Zermatt... 49

Sunnegga to Findeln: Simple and Beautiful...................................49

Moos Trail: Nature Exploration for Kids..50

Wolli Adventure Park: Fun for All Ages...52

Advanced Hiking Routes in Zermatt..55

Hohbalmen: Challenging and Rewarding.......................................55

Breithorn Ascent: High-Altitude Adventure...................................57

Hörnli Hut: Near the Matterhorn..59

Multi-Day Hiking Adventures in Zermatt..63

The Haute Route: Zermatt to Chamonix..63

Tour of Monte Rosa: Epic Mountain Journey................................65

Walker's Haute Route: Stunning Landscapes.................................67

Itinerary Suggestions for Zermatt 71

    The Three-Day Explorer 71

    The Weeklong Adventurer 72

Guided Tours and Local Guides in Zermatt 75

    Advantages of Hiring a Guide 75

    Recommended Local Guides 76

Hiking Events and Festivals in Zermatt 2024 79

    Zermatt Marathon: Test Your Limits 79

    The Gornergrat Nature Festival 80

    Matterhorn Ultraks 81

Flora and Fauna of the Swiss Alps 83

    Alpine Flowers and Plants 83

    Wildlife You Might Encounter 84

    Conservation and Responsible Hiking 84

Cultural and Historical Highlights in Zermatt and the Swiss Alps 87

    Traditional Swiss Villages 87

    Zermatt Museum: Discover Local Heritage 87

    Historic Sites Along Hiking Trails 88

Après-Hiking in Zermatt 89

    Best Places for Relaxation and Recovery 89

    Local Cuisine and Dining Recommendations 89

    Wellness and Spa Options 90

Practical Information for Hiking in Zermatt 93

Maps & Resources 93

Emergency Contacts and Services 93

Local Language Tips and Phrases 94

Medical Facilities in Zermatt 97

Personal Stories and Testimonials 101

Hikers' Experiences and Stories 101

Inspirational Hiking Journeys 101

Tips from Experienced Hikers 102

Frequently Asked Questions About Hiking In Zermatt 105

Conclusion 109

Reflecting on Your Hiking Adventures 109

Plan Your Next Trip to Zermatt 109

Final Tips and Advice 110

ZERMATT MAP

SCAN THE QR CODE

1. Open your device's camera app.
2. Point the camera at the QR code.
3. Ensure the QR code is within the frame and well-lit.
4. Wait for your device to recognize the QR code.
5. Once recognized, tap on the notification or follow the prompt to access the content or action associated with the QR code.

About This Guide

Zermatt Hiking Adventures 2024: Exploring the Swiss Alps is intended to serve as a thorough guide to one of the world's most stunning hiking locations. This handbook has been thoughtfully created to offer you all the information you need to make your hiking trip to Zermatt memorable, safe, and pleasurable. Here's a detailed look at what this guide provides:

Purpose and Scope

The major goal of this book is to provide extensive, practical information to both new hikers and experienced travelers. Whether planning a quick visit or a longer stay, this handbook will help you explore and appreciate the trails surrounding Zermatt.

- **Comprehensive Coverage:** The book provides thorough descriptions of popular hiking paths, family-friendly routes, tough hiking challenges, and multi-day expeditions. It includes everything from easy, picturesque walks to strenuous high-altitude treks, guaranteeing that hikers of all skill levels may find something acceptable.

- **Practical Advice:** It includes important information on clothing, safety precautions, weather considerations, and health preparations. This useful advice is critical for ensuring a safe and happy hiking trip, especially in the difficult alpine environment of Zermatt.

Zermatt Hiking Adventures 2024: Exploring the Swiss Alps is more than a handbook; it begins a wonderful trip to one of the world's most beautiful hiking locations. Whether you're searching for a leisurely walk or a strenuous mountain trek, this book has the tools, information, and inspiration to turn your hiking fantasies into reality. This detailed guide lets you confidently and excitedly explore Zermatt's breathtaking landscapes.

Introduction to Zermatt

Welcome to Zermatt

Zermatt, a lovely village in the Swiss Alps, has attracted visitors for years. Zermatt, known for its breathtaking alpine beauty, world-class hiking paths, and dynamic local culture, is a refuge for both outdoor enthusiasts and nature lovers. As you enter this car-free village, you are welcomed with fresh mountain air, picturesque chalets, and a warm, friendly environment that makes Zermatt a one-of-a-kind destination year-round.

Zermatt's dedication to maintaining its natural beauty and traditional Swiss charm is seen in many aspects of the village. Electric taxis and horse-drawn carriages convey guests through the tiny, cobblestone streets, preserving the peaceful atmosphere that distinguishes Zermatt from other tourist destinations. Whether you're an enthusiastic hiker searching for demanding paths or a leisure tourist hoping to take in the breathtaking scenery, Zermatt has something for everyone.

A Brief History of Zermatt

Zermatt's history is rich and diverse, showing its evolution from a secluded agricultural community to a world-famous tourist destination. The name "Zermatt" is derived from the words "zur Matte," which means "to the meadow," implying an agricultural background. For generations, Zermatt remained relatively isolated, with an economy centered on agriculture and animals.

The introduction of climbing in the mid-nineteenth century was a turning point in Zermatt's history. Edward Whymper and his team's first ascent of the Matterhorn in 1865 established Zermatt as a popular destination for climbers and explorers. Unfortunately, this ascent also marked a melancholy event in mountaineering history, since four of the seven climbers died on the descent. Despite this, the successful climb of the Matterhorn triggered a boom in curiosity and exploration, establishing Zermatt as a popular mountaineering and tourist destination.

The coming of the railway in 1891 expedited Zermatt's development and made it more accessible to tourists. Zermatt has grown into a major destination for both winter and summer activities, with elegant hotels, gourmet restaurants, and a range of cultural events, all while keeping its classic alpine charm.

Zermatt in 2024: What's New?

As we look ahead to 2024, Zermatt continues to innovate and improve the guest experience while maintaining its natural and cultural legacy. Here's an overview of what's new and interesting in Zermatt this year:

1. Sustainable Tourism Measures: Zermatt has long been a sustainability pioneer, and in 2024, the town will undertake new measures to further decrease its carbon impact. This includes increasing its network of electric transit choices, encouraging eco-friendly hotels, and improving waste management systems to guarantee that the pristine environment is preserved for future generations.

2. Trail Improvements and New Routes: For hikers, 2024 promises significant changes to Zermatt's route network. Several popular routes have been updated with greater signage, more safety precautions, and new rest stops. Furthermore, a few new routes have been added, providing new viewpoints and less congested roads for those seeking peace and adventure.

3. Cultural and Artistic Events: Zermatt's cultural environment is being enriched with a variety of events and festivals. The new Zermatt Music Festival promises to be a highlight, with concerts by worldwide performers in spectacular mountain surroundings. Art installations and exhibits featuring local and international talent are also planned, providing a colorful cultural component to your stay.

4. Improved Visitors Services: To make your stay even more enjoyable, Zermatt has renovated its visitor facilities. A new cutting-edge tourist center offers complete information, booking help, and tailored suggestions. Enhanced Wi-Fi coverage throughout the village allows you to remain connected and share your experiences with ease.

5. Gastronomic Delights: Foodies will be charmed by Zermatt's gastronomic inventions. New gourmet restaurants and menu updates at established enterprises emphasize regional foods and environmental processes. Zermatt's culinary scene is constantly evolving, providing a wide range of eating experiences, from traditional Swiss cuisine to worldwide gourmet treats.

Zermatt in 2024 is the right combination of history and modernity, providing each guest with a one-of-a-kind and memorable experience. Whether you're discovering new hiking paths, attending cultural events, or just admiring the tranquil beauty of the Alps, Zermatt promises to be an unforgettable vacation. Welcome to Zermatt, your portal to unforgettable alpine activities and lasting memories.

Geography and Climate of Zermatt

Geography

Zermatt is a scenic alpine village in southern Switzerland's Valais canton, which speaks German. Nestled at a height of around 1,620 meters (5,315 feet) above sea level, it is recognized for its breathtaking alpine landscape, which includes the iconic Matterhorn, one of the world's most famous mountains.

1. Location and Surroundings
- **Position:** Zermatt is located in the Pennine Alps, near the Italian border. The settlement is located at the upper end of the Mattertal valley, which is surrounded by some of the highest peaks in the Alps, notably Dufourspitze (4,634 meters) in the Monte Rosa massif, Switzerland's highest mountain.
- **Neighboring Areas:** The Mattertal valley connects to the greater Rhone river, which runs through the canton of Valais. To the south, the valley ends in the Theodul Pass, an ancient trade route that connects Switzerland and Italy.

2. Topography
- **Mountain Ranges:** Zermatt is bordered by a difficult mountainous topography, with over 29 peaks surpassing 4,000 meters. These include the Matterhorn (4,478 m), Weisshorn (4,506 m), and Liskamm (4,533 m).
- **Glaciers:** The region is abundant in glaciers, the Gorner Glacier being one of the biggest and most accessible. The glaciers enhance the spectacular environment and provide unique chances for glacier trekking and climbing.

3. Rivers and Lakes
- **Rivers:** The Matter Vispa River originates from the glaciers that encircle Zermatt. It flows along the Mattertal valley before joining the Saas Vispa and, finally, the Rhone River.
- **Lakes:** The area has numerous alpine lakes, including the Riffelsee, Stellisee, and Schwarzsee. These lakes are well-known for their crystal-clear waters and beautiful reflections of the surrounding peaks.

4. Paths and Accessibility
- **Hiking Path:** Zermatt offers a diverse network of hiking paths, including simple treks and strenuous high-altitude climbs. These routes provide breathtaking views of the alpine terrain and access to distant locations.
- **Accessibility:** To protect its pure nature, Zermatt has no cars. Visitors often come by rail, with the picturesque Matterhorn Gotthard Bahn serving as the last

part of their trip. In Zermatt, the principal sources of transportation are electric taxis, buses, and bicycles.

Climate

Zermatt has a high-altitude alpine climate that varies greatly depending on the season and altitude. Understanding the local climate is essential for planning a safe and pleasurable trip.

1. Temperature
- **Summer (June to August):** Zermatt has pleasant summers, with daily temperatures ranging from 10°C to 20°C (50°F to 68°F) at the village level. However, temperatures may decrease dramatically at higher elevations, particularly in the early morning and late evening.
- **Winter (December to February):** The town experiences frigid weather, with typical daily temperatures ranging from -10°C to 0°C. At higher altitudes, temperatures may drop far below freezing, typically accompanied by strong winds.

2. Precipitation
- **Rainfall:** Zermatt has modest rainfall throughout the year, with a little increase during summer owing to afternoon thunderstorms. The annual precipitation average is 700-800 millimeters (28-32 inches).
- **Snowfall:** Snowfall is an important characteristic of the Zermatt climate, especially between November and April. The village and surrounding mountains are often covered with snow, providing great conditions for winter sports and alpine activities.

3. Sunlight
- **Sunlight Hours:** Zermatt receives plenty of sunlight, especially during the summer months. The high altitude and bright sky lead to an average of over 2,000 hours of sunlight each year. Due to reduced daylight hours and frequent snowfalls, there are fewer bright days throughout the winter months.

4. Seasonal Variations
- **Spring (March-May):** Zermatt experiences progressively increasing temperatures and snowmelt. It's a transitional phase, with some paths becoming accessible and others remaining snow-covered.

- **Autumn (September to November):** This season provides colder temperatures and gorgeous autumn foliage. It's a calmer season with fewer people, which makes it excellent for trekking and admiring the changing scenery.

5. Microclimates
- **Altitude Effects:** Zermatt's climate changes substantially based on height. While the village has relatively pleasant temperatures, higher elevations are substantially colder and more susceptible to rapid weather changes.
- **Glacial Influence:** The existence of glaciers influences the local climate, resulting in colder temperatures and unique weather patterns in certain places.

Impact on Hiking

The hiking experience in Zermatt is heavily influenced by its landscape and climate.

1. Trail Conditions
- **Summer Hiking:** Most trails are accessible and free of snow, making it the ideal season for hiking. Hikers should still be prepared for unexpected weather changes and lower temperatures at higher altitudes.
- **Winter and Early Spring Hiking:** Winter and early spring treks need specialist equipment, such as crampons and ice axes, and should be done under the supervision of an experienced climber.

2. Weather Considerations
- **Layering:** Layering is necessary due to the unpredictable environment. Hikers should be ready for both bright, sunny weather and unexpected cold snaps or rain showers.
- **Weather Monitoring:** It is vital to monitor weather predictions and local circumstances. Mountain weather may change quickly, so hikers should be prepared to adapt their plans appropriately.

3. Safety and Preparedness
- **Altitude Sickness:** High heights increase the danger of altitude sickness. Acclimatization, keeping hydrated, and detecting symptoms are essential for a healthy hiking trip.
- **Emergency Preparedness:** Hikers should have a first-aid kit, enough food and water, and emergency contact information for mountain rescue agencies.

Zermatt's terrain and temperature are distinguishing characteristics that make it a top choice for hikers and outdoor lovers. The stunning landscapes, dominated by towering peaks and pristine glaciers, provide a wide range of trekking opportunities, from strolls to strenuous alpine climbs. Understanding the local climate and geographical factors is critical to planning a safe and fun excursion. Hikers who are properly equipped and knowledgeable may truly enjoy Zermatt's natural beauty and unique difficulties.

Planning Your Zermatt Hiking Adventure

Research and Preparation

1. Gather Information
- **Guidebooks and Maps:** Get detailed guidebooks and topographic maps of Zermatt. These resources provide essential information on trails, difficulty levels, and areas of interest.
- **Online Resources:** Use websites and forums devoted to hiking in Zermatt. Platforms such as the Zermatt Tourism website provide route descriptions, current conditions, and suggestions.
- **Local contacts:** Contact your local hiking groups or guides for personal information and ideas. They may give vital information on trail conditions and seasonal changes.

2. Choosing the Right Time
- **Seasonal Considerations:** Zermatt provides diverse hiking experiences throughout the year. The greatest season to go trekking is from late June to early September when most paths are clear of snow and the weather is consistent.
- **Weather Patterns:** Be mindful of the weather conditions during your intended stay. Summer months may still bring unexpected storms, so check the weather and plan appropriately.

Planning Your Itinerary

1. Trail Selection
- **Variety of Trails:** Zermatt provides a diverse choice of paths, including simple walks and challenging alpine treks. Choose paths that match your fitness level and interests. Popular choices include the Five Lakes Walk, Gornergrat, and the Matterhorn Trail.
- **Trail Information:** Look up trail lengths, elevation increases, and expected time of completion. This information allows you to arrange your days more effectively and avoid overcommitting.

2. Day-by-Day Planning
- **Balanced Itinerary:** Schedule a balance of hiking and relaxation days. This helps your body to recuperate and lowers the likelihood of overexertion.
- **Local Attractions:** Visit the Zermatt Museum, Glacier Palace, and classic Swiss villages. These provide cultural lessons and a respite from trekking.

3. Accommodation
- **Advance Booking:** Book in early, particularly during peak hiking season. Luxury hotels, mountain huts, and campsites are among the lodging options.
- **Location:** Look for accommodations that are close to trailheads or have easy access to transit. The majority of treks are best done from Zermatt town.

Final Preparations

1. Packing list
- **Checklists:** Use a packing list to ensure you don't forget anything important. Double-check your equipment, clothes, and food.
- **Packing Efficiently:** Pack effectively to achieve a balance of weight and accessibility. Keep regularly used things in easy-access pockets.

2. Last-Minute Checks
- **Weather Update:** Check the weather forecast before heading out each day.
- **Trail Conditions:** Check the trail conditions and any possible closures or dangers.

3. Mental Preparation
- **Stay Positive:** Maintain a positive mindset and adapt to adversities. Hiking might be unexpected, but keeping a cheerful attitude can help you enjoy the experience.
- **Enjoy the Journey:** Remember to take in the breathtaking landscape, breathe fresh mountain air, and enjoy nature's beauty.

Planning your hiking trip in Zermatt requires thorough planning and study. You may ensure a safe and pleasurable trip by acquiring information, choosing the appropriate equipment, comprehending safety requirements, and preparing physically and emotionally. Whether you're going on a short vacation or a week-long adventure, rigorous preparation helps you to completely immerse yourself in the stunning beauty and unique difficulties of the Swiss Alps.

Preparing For Your Zermatt Hiking Adventure

Essential Gear and Equipment

Hiking in Zermatt's breathtaking scenery requires meticulous planning to guarantee comfort, safety, and pleasure. Here's a comprehensive introduction to the important gear and equipment you'll need.

1. Clothing
- **Layering System:** Layering is essential for trekking in the Swiss Alps. Start with a breathable base layer to keep perspiration off your skin. For extra warmth, add an insulating layer like a fleece or down jacket. Finally, protect yourself from the elements by wearing a waterproof and windproof outer layer.
- **Hiking Pants and Shorts:** Lightweight, quick-drying pants work well for most treks. Convertible trousers that can be zipped down into shorts are ideal for changing climates.
- **Hiking socks:** High-quality, moisture-wicking socks assist you avoid blisters and keep your feet comfy. Consider taking an extra pair in case they get wet.
- **Footwear:** To navigate rough and uneven terrain, choose sturdy, well-fitted hiking boots with strong ankle support and grip. To prevent blisters, ensure they have been broken in before your journey.
- **Hat and Gloves:** A wide-brimmed hat gives sun protection, while a beanie and gloves are required for cooler weather.

2. Backpack
- **Daypack:** For day treks, a 20-30 liter backpack is suitable. It should include comfortable straps, a waist belt, and many pockets to keep your goods organized.
- **Hydration System:** Many backpacks have built-in hydration bladder chambers. Alternatively, bring water bottles to remain hydrated on your trek.

3. Navigation Tools
- **Map and Compass:** Carry a thorough map and compass. Familiarize yourself with their usage to ensure safe navigation.
- **GPS Device or Smartphone:** A GPS device or a smartphone with offline maps may be quite useful for navigating. Make sure it's completely charged, and carry a portable charger.

4. Safety and First Aid
- **First Aid Kit:** Pack a first aid kit with bandages, antiseptic wipes, blister treatment, pain relievers, and personal prescriptions.

- **Emergency Shelter:** If you are stuck out overnight, a lightweight emergency blanket or bivy sack may give some protection.
- **Multi-tool or Knife:** A multi-tool or knife may be used for many activities, such as cutting food and fixing gear.
- **Whistle:** If you are in difficulty, use a whistle to signal for aid.

5. Lighting
- **Headlamp of Flashlight:** Bring a headlamp or flashlight for unforeseen delays, even if you're not hiking at night. Bring some extra batteries.

6. Food and Water
- **Hydration:** Bring enough water to last the trek, and consider using a water filter or purification tablets if you want to refresh from natural sources.
- **Snacks and Meals:** Carry high-energy foods like almonds, dried fruit, and energy bars. For longer walks, carry light lunches that are simple to cook.

7. Additional Gear
- **Trekking Poles:** Trekking poles provide stability and prevent knee pain, particularly on steep or uneven terrain.
- **Sunglasses and Sunscreen:** Wear sunglasses to protect your eyes from UV radiation, and apply sunscreen to any exposed skin to avoid sunburn.
- **Camera or Smartphone:** Record the breathtaking scenery and unforgettable moments of your walk.

Safety Tips and Guidelines.

When trekking in Zermatt, safety should always come first. Here are detailed safety precautions to guarantee a safe and pleasurable hiking experience:

1. Plan Ahead
- **Research Your Route:** Examine your preferred hiking path, including mileage, elevation gain, and difficulty level. Check for recent trail conditions or closures.
- **Inform Others:** Tell someone about your trekking intentions, including your planned return time. This is critical in case of an emergency.

2. Check weather Conditions
- **Forecast:** Always check the weather forecast before going out. Be prepared for unexpected weather changes, which are prevalent in mountainous places.
- **Avoid Dangerous Conditions:** Avoid trekking during thunderstorms, strong gusts, or heavy rain. Lightning is very deadly in mountainous environments.

3. Stick to Marked Trails
- **Follow Trail Markers:** To prevent getting lost, stick to designated routes and obey trail signs. Going off-trail might result in perilous terrain and environmental harm.
- **Respectful Signage:** Pay heed to warning signs and path closures. These are in place to ensure your safety.

4. Pace Yourself
- **Know Your Limits:** Choose paths based on your fitness level and expertise. Do not overexert yourself, and take rests as required.
- **Hydrate and Eat:** To stay energized, drink plenty of fluids and munch on high-energy foods.

5. Be Wildlife Aware
- **Respect Wildlife:** Observe animals from a distance and avoid feeding them. To prevent attracting animals, store food securely.
- **Bear Precautions:** If trekking in locations where bears are prevalent, bring bear spray and know how to use it. Make noise to avoid startling the animals.

6. Emergency Preparedness
- **Know Emergency Contacts:** Familiarize yourself with local emergency numbers and rescue service locations.
- **Carry a First Aid Kit:** Be prepared to treat small injuries and understand basic first aid methods.

7. Altitude Awareness
- **Acclimatize:** Allow for acclimatization if unfamiliar with high heights. Altitude sickness symptoms include dizziness, nausea, and headaches.
- **Descend if Necessary:** If you encounter severe symptoms of altitude sickness, descend to a lower height right away.

8. Leave No Trace
- **Pack Out Waste:** Pack out your rubbish and properly dispose of it. Leave natural and historical items alone.
- **Minimize Impact:** Use durable surfaces, minimize trampling plants, and respect animal habitats.

Weather Considerations

The weather in the Swiss Alps may be unpredictable, so be prepared for a variety of circumstances. Here's a comprehensive reference on weather considerations for your hiking trip in Zermatt:

1. Seasonal Variations
- **Spring (April to June):** Mild weather and blossoming mountain flowers are the hallmarks of spring. Higher altitudes may still have snow, and the weather might be erratic. Dress in layers and ready for rainy weather.
- **Summer (July to September):** This is the prime hiking season, with higher temperatures and longer days. Afternoon thunderstorms are typical, so plan your walks early and be prepared for unexpected weather changes.
- **Fall (October to November):** Enjoy milder temperatures and stunning fall hues. Although the trails may be less busy, early snowfall is likely at higher altitudes.
- **Winter (December to March):** Hiking is more difficult owing to snow and low weather. Specialized equipment, such as snowshoes or crampons, and previous familiarity with winter conditions are required.

2. Daily Weather Patterns
- **Morning:** Mornings are often cooler and quieter, so they are the ideal time to begin your journey. Visibility is generally greater in the morning.
- **Afternoon:** Afternoons might bring more cloud cover, thunderstorms, and shifting weather. Plan to arrive at your destination or return by early afternoon.

3. Temperature Considerations
- **Layering:** Temperatures may fluctuate dramatically during the day and as elevation changes. Dress in layers to adapt to changing situations.
- **Wind Chill:** Wind may drastically reduce felt temperature, particularly at higher altitudes. Bring a windproof jacket and thick clothes.

4. Rainfall and Thunderstorms
- **Rain Gear:** Always bring a waterproof jacket and trousers, even if the weather prediction is clear. Sudden rain showers are prevalent in mountainous places.
- **Storm Safety:** During a thunderstorm, avoid exposed peaks and summits. Seek cover at lower elevations and wait for the storm to pass.

5. Sun Protection
- **UV Exposure:** UV rays are more intense at higher elevations. Wear sunscreen, sunglasses, and a wide-brimmed hat to avoid sunburn.

- **Hydration:** Sun and altitude may lead to dehydration. Drink lots of water while you trek.

6. Snow and Ice
- **Snowfields:** Exercise caution while crossing snowfields, particularly in early summer when snow may still be visible. Use hiking poles and proper boots.
- **Avalanche Risk:** Be cautious of avalanche threats throughout the winter and spring. Check local avalanche predictions and avoid high-risk locations.

Health and Fitness Preparations

Proper health and fitness preparation are essential for a successful and pleasurable hiking trip in Zermatt. Here's a detailed guide to getting fit and keeping healthy on the trails:

1. Physical Conditioning
- **Cardiovascular Fitness:** Improve your cardiovascular fitness via sports like jogging, cycling, and swimming. Aim for at least 30 minutes of moderate to intense activity three to five days per week.
- **Strength Training:** Use strength training routines to increase muscular endurance, especially in your legs and core. Squats, lunges, and step-ups are good exercises for hikers.
- **Flexibility and Balance:** Stretching exercises and yoga-style activities may help you improve your flexibility and balance. This reduces damage and enhances stability on rough terrain.

2. Endurance Training
- **Hiking Practice:** Gradually increase distance and height during practice treks. Begin with shorter, less strenuous treks then progress to longer, more difficult terrain. This increases endurance and prepares your body for the challenges of trekking in the Alps.

3. Altitude Acclimatization
- **Gradual Ascent:** Spend a few days at a higher level before tackling more challenging excursions. This helps your body to acclimate to the thinner air, lowering the risk of altitude sickness.
- **Stay Hydrated:** Drink lots of water to help your body adapt to the effects of altitude. Avoid excessive alcohol and coffee, which may lead to dehydration.

4. Nutrition
- **Balanced Diet:** Maintain a balanced diet with carbs, proteins, and healthy fats to power your body while trekking. Concentrate on healthy foods including fruits, vegetables, lean meats, and whole grains.

5. Health Check-Up
- **Medical Clearance:** Before trekking, talk with your doctor about any existing medical illnesses or concerns. Make sure you're physically fit enough to handle the hardships of high-altitude trekking.
- **Vaccines and Medications:** Make sure you have all of the essential vaccines. Carry any personal prescriptions you may need, and consider altitude sickness medication if you are prone to symptoms.

6. Mental Preparation
- **Positive Attitude:** Maintain a happy and open mentality throughout your hiking excursion. Being psychologically prepared for hardships and being hopeful may significantly improve your whole experience.
- **Mindfulness and Relaxation:** Use mindfulness or relaxation methods to reduce stress and maintain concentration. Deep breathing, meditation, or simple visualization techniques may be effective.

7. Emergency Preparedness
- **Emergency Plan:** Create a clear emergency plan. Know where the closest emergency services are and how to call them. Bring a map with emergency shelters and exits noted.
- **Buddy System:** If feasible, hike with a buddy or a group. If you're hiking alone, let someone know your intentions and when you anticipate to return. Solo hikers should be very careful and well-prepared.

8. Practice and Preparation
- **Local Hikes:** Begin with local treks that imitate the conditions of Zermatt routes. This enables you to test your equipment and gain confidence.
- **Height Gains:** Gradually increase the height gain on your practice climbs to mimic the altitude fluctuations you will encounter in Zermatt.

By following these detailed preparations, you'll be well-prepared to tackle Zermatt's stunning and demanding hiking paths. Taking the time to properly prepare means that you can completely appreciate the stunning landscape and unique experiences that this alpine wonderland has to offer.

Getting to Zermatt

Travel Options to Zermatt

Zermatt, situated in the Swiss canton of Valais, is famous for its breathtaking alpine landscape and the iconic Matterhorn. Despite its isolated position, Zermatt is readily accessible through a variety of transportation modes.

1. By Train
- **Swiss Federal Railways (SBB):** This offers the most popular and picturesque route to Zermatt by rail. Swiss Federal Railways (SBB) provides frequent service from major cities like Zurich, Geneva, and Bern. The trains are timely, pleasant, and provide spectacular views of the Swiss landscape.
- **Glacier Express:** For a really unforgettable voyage, take the Glacier Express, dubbed the "slowest express train in the world." This luxury train travels from St. Moritz/Davos to Zermatt, traveling through breathtaking vistas such as the Rhine Gorge and the Oberalp Pass. The ride lasts around eight hours and provides panoramic vistas through its big windows.
- **Local Trains:** Transfer from Visp or Brig to Matterhorn Gotthard Bahn (MGB) for the last leg to Zermatt. The narrow-gauge cogwheel train winds through the valley, affording breathtaking views as it ascends.

2. By Car
- **Driving to Täsch:** Travel by automobile to Täsch, the final settlement before Zermatt. From there, it's a 5-kilometer drive to Zermatt, a car-free zone.
- **Parking in Täsch:** There are many parking lots accessible in Täsch where you may keep your car. The Matterhorn Terminal Täsch is a handy choice, with covered parking and luggage delivery to your Zermatt hotel.
- **Shuttle Train from Täsch:** The Matterhorn Gotthard Bahn shuttle train departs Täsch every 20 minutes and travels to Zermatt in about 12 minutes.

3. By Air
- **Closest Airport:** The closest international airports to Zermatt are Zurich Airport (ZRH) and Geneva Airport (GVA), which are around three to four hours distant by rail. Smaller airports, such as Sion (SIR) and Bern (BRN), provide relatively restricted services.
- **Transfers from Airports:** Once you arrive at the airport, you may simply transfer to the rail services that link to Zermatt. Swiss Federal Railways provide regular connections from Zurich and Geneva airports.

4. By Bus
- **Long-Distance Buses:** While less prevalent than railroads, long-distance bus services from adjacent countries or Swiss cities exist. These buses usually drop off passengers at Visp or Täsch, where they may board the train for the last trip to Zermatt.

5. Private Transfers and Helicopters
- **Private Car Services:** For a more customized experience, private car services and taxis provide door-to-door transportation from major Swiss towns and airports to Täsch or Zermatt.
- **Helicopter Transfers:** Helicopter transfers from Swiss airports to Zermatt provide a really unique and luxurious arrival experience. This service is provided by companies such as Air Zermatt and offers a wonderful aerial perspective of the Alps.

Transportation in Zermatt

Zermatt's dedication to sustainability is reflected in its transportation policy. As a car-free community, Zermatt provides a variety of environmentally friendly transit choices to assist guests get about comfortably and effectively.

1. Electric Taxis
- **Availability:** These are a common method of transportation in Zermatt. They are widely accessible and may be hailed on the street or reserved in advance.
- **Convenience:** These taxis are especially excellent for moving baggage from the train station to your hotel or making brief visits throughout the hamlet.

2. Horse-Drawn Carriages
- **Scenic Rides:** These are a charming and scenic way to see Zermatt. They provide a leisurely tour around the village, enabling you to take in the wonderful atmosphere and natural splendor.
- **Reservations:** Carriage rides may be scheduled through local suppliers or at hotels and tourist information centers.

3. Electric Buses
- **Routes:** Zermatt has a fleet of electric buses that operate on several routes across the resort. These buses are environmentally friendly and provide a handy method to go throughout the region, particularly for those staying in more remote hotels.

- **Schedules:** Buses run frequently, providing low wait periods. Timetables are accessible at bus stations and visitor information centers.

4. Walking and Cycling
- **Pedestrian-Friendly:** Zermatt is a pedestrian-friendly village with well-kept walkways and trails. Walking is the greatest way to explore the little streets, go shopping, and enjoy the local cafés and eateries.
- **Bicycle Rentals:** Bicycles and e-bikes are available for hire at many stores around the village. Cycling is a terrific way to get about and explore the surrounding places and trails.

5. Gornergrat Railway
- **Scenic Railway:** A cogwheel train transports guests from Zermatt to the peak. This excursion provides amazing panoramic views of the Matterhorn and its neighboring peaks.

Hiking Access: The railway provides easy access to hiking trails and high-altitude routes, making it an important component of the Zermatt experience.

6. Sunnegga Funicular
- **Underground Funicular:** The underground funicular offers fast and simple access to the Sunnegga paradise, which serves as a starting point for several hiking paths. The funicular runs through a tunnel and provides breathtaking vistas upon arrival.

Accommodation Options

Zermatt has a variety of hotel alternatives to suit all budgets and interests. Whether you choose to stay in a fancy hotel, a quiet chalet, or a budget-friendly hostel, Zermatt has it all.

1. Luxury Hotels

- **The Omnia (Address: Auf dem Fels, 3920 Zermatt, Switzerland)**

The Omnia is a magnificent resort hotel located on a cliff above Zermatt, Switzerland. It boasts beautiful rooms and suites, a spa, an indoor pool, and a fitness center, as well as stunning views of the Matterhorn Peak. The hotel is near the main train station and has easy access to Zermatt's retail and eating districts. Guests may engage in a variety of sports in the neighboring mountains, including skiing, snowboarding, and hiking. The

Omnia Zermatt is well-known for its great service and magnificent design, making it a favorite option among couples and families.

- **Mont Cervin Palace (Address: Bahnhofstrasse 31, 3920 Zermatt, Switzerland)**

The 5-star luxury hotel is situated in Zermatt, Switzerland. It provides spectacular views of the majestic Matterhorn. The hotel offers luxurious rooms, great restaurants, and a variety of wellness and leisure amenities. Guests staying at this prominent mountain resort may explore the gorgeous town of Zermatt as well as the surrounding Swiss Alps.

- **Riffelalp Resort 2222m (Address: Mark Twain Weg, Zermatt 3920 Switzerland)**

Situated 2,222 meters above sea level, the Riffelalp Resort 2222m is a five-star hotel located in Zermatt, Switzerland. It provides amazing views of the Matterhorn and other Swiss Alps. The resort offers upscale facilities such as a spa, various dining choices, and a range of outdoor activities. It also provides easy access to hiking routes.

2. Mid-Range Hotels

- **Hotel Alpenhof (Address: Matterstrasse 43, 3920 Zermatt, Switzerland)**

The family-run Hotel Alpenhof is located in the heart of Zermatt, in a sunny and peaceful setting. It has spectacular views of the Matterhorn and is a short walk from the town center. The cable car Sunnegga, which accesses the ski slopes and hiking area, is just across from the hotel, while the train station and Gornergrat railway are only a 5-minute walk away. The hotel offers pleasant rooms and suites, each with contemporary facilities and a balcony. Guests may engage in a variety of sports, including skiing, snowboarding, and hiking, as well as rest in the hotel's spa and wellness center. The hotel's restaurant provides exquisite Swiss cuisine and has a pleasant bar with a fireplace.

- **Hotel Daniela (Address: Steinmattstrasse 39, 3920 Zermatt, Switzerland)**

The Hotel Daniela is small, but it has many things to offer. it is Located in a calm area and it's about 10 minutes from the ski lifts and train station. It has luxury rooms and suites with breathtaking views of the Matterhorn. The hotel offers free breakfast, and convenient access to hiking trail. Hotel Daniela is ideal for those looking for a quiet escape from the stunning Swiss Alps backdrop.

- **Hotel Butterfly (Address: Bodmenstrasse 21, 3920 Zermatt, Switzerland)**

Hotel Butterfly is a charming gem tucked in the car-free town center. With its superb position only 150 meters from the train station and the famed Matterhorn as a background, it's an excellent starting point for sightseeing. The hotel has comfortable accommodations, a wonderful restaurant, and a wellness area with a Finnish sauna, infrared cabin, steam bath, and tanning bed.

3. Budget-Friendly Options

- **Youth Hostel Zermatt (Address: Am Stalden 5, 3920 Zermatt, Switzerland)**

The Zermatt Youth Hostel provides an economical and lovely option for tourists looking for a comfortable base in this high-alpine resort. With unrestricted views of the world-famous Matterhorn, also known locally as the "Horu". The hostel, located within a 10-minute walk from the ski lifts and Zermatt's city center, offers a variety of lodging choices, including private bathrooms, shared amenities, and dormitory beds.

- **Hotel Alphubel (Address: Brantschenhaus 7, 3920 Zermatt, Switzerland)**

Hotel Alphubel is suitable for budget-conscious guests seeking pleasant accommodations. It is about 200 meters from the Gornergrat Mountain Railway and the Zermatt Train Station. Guests may also enjoy the sauna and the on-site restaurant. The Alpine-style rooms feature private bathrooms, and the majority have balconies.

4. Chalets & Apartments
- **Chalet Ulysses (Address: Staldenstrasse 112, 3920 Zermatt, Switzerland)**

The Chalet Ulysse was constructed in 2009 in the typical Swiss Chalet style with plenty of wood and has two lovely furnished flats. It is situated just across from the Winkelmatten bus stop, with two excellent family restaurants and a convenient grocery shop nearby. Just opposite the chalet, there is a children's playground. It also offers breathtaking Matterhorn views and it is ideal for families with children.

- **Mountain Exposure (Address: Schälpmattgasse 14, 3920 Zermatt, Switzerland)**

Mountain Exposure specializes in luxury chalet rentals and provides a variety of tastefully outfitted chalets and apartments with customized services.
This service includes transfer arrangements, ski passes, child care, ski equipment rentals, and meal reservations.

- **Haus Mischabel (Address: Hofmattstrasse 20, 3920 Zermatt, Switzerland)**

The Haus Mischabel is located in a central, sunny area. Bordering Zermatt's ancient Hinterdorf neighborhood, a 5-minute walk from the train station, and near to a bus stop, restaurants, sports stores, and other businesses. For a more private and homely experience, Haus Mischabel also offers fully furnished apartments with kitchens, which are excellent for families or extended visits.

5. Boutique Hotels
- **Hotel Matterhorn Focus (Address: Schluhmattstrasse 131, 3920 Zermatt, Switzerland)**

Matterhorn Focus is located in a unique position, immediately across from the "Matterhorn glacier paradise" valley station. If you want to trek and ski all day, here is the perfect place to start. In addition, you can walk to the village center in less than 10 minutes. It is a design hotel with contemporary construction and trendy furnishings, offering panoramic views, an indoor pool, and a spa.

- **Backstage Hotel Vernissage (Address: Hofmattstrasse 4, 3920 Zermatt, Switzerland)**

Backstage Hotel Vernissage is a wonderful alternative for visitors to Zermatt, providing a romantic setting and various useful services to make your stay more enjoyable. The hotel has a concierge and room service, as well as a heated jacuzzi and complimentary breakfast, which will provide a welcome break from your hectic day. Backstage Hotel Vernissage makes it simple to explore some wonderful Zermatt sights, such as the iconic Bergführerdenkmal.

6. Eco-Friendly Accommodations
- **Cervo Mountain Resort (Address: Riedweg 156, 3920 Zermatt, Switzerland)**

This is committed to sustainability, providing eco-friendly rooms, organic eating alternatives, and limiting its environmental impact.

- **Hotel Alpenblick (Address: Oberdorfstrasse 106, 3920 Zermatt, Switzerland)**

Hotel Alpenblick is an environmentally aware hotel with a strong focus on sustainability. It offers comfortable accommodations, a solar-powered sauna, and organic cuisine choices.

Whether you choose the utmost in luxury or a warm and economical place to stay, Zermatt's numerous lodging choices will assure a pleasant and memorable stay in the gorgeous Swiss Alps.

Top Hiking Trails in Zermatt

Gornergrat: A Panoramic Adventure

The Gornergrat route in Zermatt provides excellent panoramic views of the Matterhorn, Monte Rosa, and the Gorner Glacier. This trek is ideal for people looking for high-altitude excitement mixed with reasonably easy terrain.

Route Details
- **Starting point:** Zermatt or the Gornergrat Railway Station.
- **Distance:** About 12 kilometers (7.5 miles).
- **Elevation Gain:** Approximately 1,500 meters (4,921 feet).
- **Difficulty:** Moderate
- **Duration:** 4-5 hours.

Highlights

- **Gornergrat Railway:** Take the picturesque Gornergrat Railway from Zermatt to reach the top. This cogwheel train trip is an adventure in itself, with breathtaking vistas as it ascends.

- **Panoramic Views:** At the Gornergrat summit (3,089 meters or 10,135 feet), take in a 360-degree vista of 29 peaks over 4,000 meters, including the renowned Matterhorn.

- **Gorner Glacier:** The path follows the crest, affording breathtaking views of the Gorner Glacier, one of the biggest and most picturesque in the Alps.

- **Observatory:** Get an astronomical perspective on the sky by visiting the Kulmhotel Gornergrat, the tallest hotel in the Swiss Alps, and the adjoining observatory.

Tips
- **Early Start:** Start early to avoid crowds and enjoy the beautiful morning sky.

- **Weather Gear:** At high elevations, the weather may change suddenly, so bring a waterproof jacket and layers.
- **Hydration and Foods:** Bring lots of water and high-energy foods to stay energized throughout the trek.

The Matterhorn Trail: Iconic Views

The Matterhorn Trail is a must-do walk for visitors to Zermatt. This trek boasts some of the greatest views of the Matterhorn, the most iconic peak in the Alps, and is a fairly difficult climb through magnificent alpine terrain.

Route Details
- **Starting Point:** Start in Schwarzsee, accessible by cable car from Zermatt.
- **Distance:** About 10 kilometers (6.2 miles).

35

- **Elevation Gain:** Approximately 400 meters (1,312 feet).
- **Difficulty:** Moderate
- **Duration:** 3-4 hours.

Highlights

- **Schwarzsee:** Start your trek at the Schwarzsee (Black Lake), which reflects the Matterhorn on calm days, making for an excellent picture opportunity.

- **Matterhorn Views:** The walk provides uninterrupted views of the Matterhorn, with various vantage locations to pause and admire its magnificence.

- **Alpine Flora and Fauna:** The track winds through rich alpine meadows brimming with wildflowers, where you could see marmots, chamois, and other species.

- **Historical Sites:** Go to the modest chapel of "Maria zum Schnee" (Mary of the Snow), a pilgrimage destination near Schwarzsee.

Tips

- **Photography:** Bring a camera or smartphone to record breathtaking vistas of the Matterhorn.
- **Comfortable Footwear:** Wear sturdy hiking boots since certain sections of the terrain might be rough and uneven.
- **Weather Awareness:** Check the weather forecast and be ready for unexpected changes, since circumstances surrounding the Matterhorn are unpredictable.

Five Lakes Walk: Scenic Beauty

The Five Lakes Walk is a popular and attractive climb in Zermatt. This walk leads you past five magnificent alpine lakes, each with its own character and offering breathtaking views of the Matterhorn.

Route Details
- **Starting Point:** Begin at Blauherd, accessible by Sunnegga funicular and Blauherd cable car.
- **Distance:** About 9.3 kilometers (5.8 miles).
- **Elevation Gain:** Approximately 500 meters (1,640 feet).
- **Difficulty:** Moderate
- **Duration:** 3-4 hours.

Highlights

- **Stellisee:** The first lake, Stellisee, is famed for its beautiful reflection of the Matterhorn, particularly between dawn and sunset.

- **Grindjisee:** Surrounded by a diverse range of alpine flora, Grindjisee provides a peaceful location for a rest.

- **Grünsee:** Grünsee, or Green Lake, is set in a more harsh, rocky terrain, offering a unique view of the alpine scenery.

- **Moosjisee:** Moosjisee is known for its turquoise hue caused by glacier meltwater, which contrasts attractively with the surrounding flora.

- **Leisee:** The last lake, Leisee, is ideal for a refreshing plunge and has family-friendly amenities, including a playground.

Tips
- **Swimming Gear:** Bring a swimsuit and towel for swimming in Leisee.

- **Picnic:** Bring a picnic to enjoy by one of the lakes, since there are sev[eral] picturesque areas to relax and take in the sights.
- **Sunscreen:** Since the route is exposed to the sun, wear sunscreen and a hat to protect yourself from UV radiation.

Zmutt: Historic and Picturesque

Zmutt Map

SCAN THE QR CODE

1. Open your device's camera app.
2. Point the camera at the QR code.
3. Ensure the QR code is within the frame and well-lit.
4. Wait for your device to recognize the QR code.
5. Once recognized, tap on the notification or follow the prompt to access the content or action associated with the QR code.

The climb to Zmutt combines history, culture, and natural beauty. This lovely village, only a short distance from Zermatt, offers trekkers a look into traditional Swiss alpine culture.

Route Details
- **Start Point:** Zermatt town center
- **Distance:** Approximately 7 kilometers (4.3 miles) round trip
- **Elevation Gain:** 350 meters (1,148 feet)
- **Difficulty:** Easy to Moderate
- **Duration:** 2-3 hours.

Highlights

- **Zmutt Town:** A historic mountain town with typical wooden chalets and barns, some from the 16th century.

- **Matterhorn Views:** The hike provides superb views of the Matterhorn and its neighboring peaks.

- **Historic Pathways:** Follow historic mule pathways that have been utilized for ages by local farmers and tradesmen.

- **Zmutt Glacier:** Admire the views of the Zmutt Glacier and the surrounding mountainous environment.

Tips
- **Historic Interest:** Explore the village and learn about its history. Some structures feature plaques with historical information.

- **Easy Access:** This trek is ideal for families and anyone seeking a shorter, less demanding climb.
- **Refreshments:** Visit one of Zmutt's classic mountain eateries for a drink or a meal.

Edelweissweg: Flower-filled Paths

The Edelweissweg, often known as the Edelweiss Trail, is a scenic stroll through flower-filled meadows with stunning views of the surrounding mountains, including the Matterhorn.

Route Details
- **Starting Point:** Begin at Blauherd, accessible by Sunnegga funicular and Blauherd cable car.
- **Distance:** About 8 kilometers (5 miles).
- **Elevation Gain:** around 450 meters (1,476 feet).
- **Difficulty:** Moderate
- **Duration:** 3-4 hours.

Highlights

- **Floral Beauty:** The route is called for the famed Edelweiss flower, which may be viewed together with other alpine flowers.

- **Panoramic Vistas:** Take in vistas of the Matterhorn, Weisshorn, and other peaks.

- **Wildlife Spotting:** Keep a look out for marmots and ibexes, which are often observed in this region.

- **Quiet Environment:** This path is less popular, providing a peaceful hiking experience.

Tips
- **Flower Guide:** Identify alpine flowers using a guidebook or app.
- **Photography:** This path is ideal for photographers, so bring your camera to capture the brilliant colors and breathtaking scenery.
- **Rest Stops:** Several benches and rest places along the path, ideal for a picnic or a respite.

Glacier Trail: Ice and Adventure

The Glacier Trail in Zermatt provides an interesting journey through the cold scenery. This track offers a close-up view of glaciers and spectacular ice formations, providing for an unforgettable and thrilling experience.

Route Details
- **Starting Point:** Start at Trockener Steg, accessible by cable car from Zermatt.
- **Distance:** About 6 kilometers (3.7 miles).
- **Elevation Gain:** around 300 meters (984 ft).
- **Difficulty:** Moderate to challenging.
- **Duration:** 3-4 hours.

Highlights

- **Glacier Views:** The hike provides stunning views of the Theodul Glacier and other ice fields.

- **Ice Formations:** See amazing ice formations, crevasses, and seracs up close.

- **Educational Information:** Several information boards along the path describe glacial dynamics and how climate change affects these ice giants.

- **Mountain Scenery:** Admire panoramic views of the surrounding peaks, including the Matterhorn and Monte Rosa.

Tips

- **Proper Gear:** Wear sturdy footwear with strong grip and consider crampons for ice weather.
- **Guide Services:** For safety reasons, consider hiring a mountain guide, particularly if you are unfamiliar with glacial terrain.
- **Weather Check:** Glacial locations may be dangerous in bad weather, so check the forecast and trail conditions before venturing out.

Each of these pathways provides a distinct experience while highlighting the diversity and spectacular beauty of Zermatt's alpine setting. Whether you want panoramic vistas, historical charm, floral beauty, or ice adventures, Zermatt offers a path that will leave you with lasting memories.

Family Friendly Hikes in Zermatt

Sunnegga to Findeln: Simple and Beautiful

The climb from Sunnegga to Findeln is ideal for families, with easy terrain and breathtaking vistas. This trip is great for families with small children and anyone looking for a relaxing, picturesque stroll in the Swiss Alps.

Route Details
- **Starting Point:** Sunnegga (accessible by funicular from Zermatt).
- **Distance:** About 2.5 kilometers (1.5 miles).
- **Elevation Gain:** Minimal
- **Difficulty:** Easy
- **Duration:** 1–2 hours

Highlights

- **Sunnegga Paradise:** Begin your trek in Sunnegga, the family-friendly "Sun Terrace" of Zermatt. Enjoy panoramic views of the Matterhorn and its neighboring peaks.

- **Leisee:** One of the highlights of this trek is Leisee, a stunning lake ideal for a family picnic. Summertime activities include BBQ spaces, a playground, and possibilities for a refreshing swim.

- **Alpine Flora and Wildlife:** The route is well-marked and provides several opportunities to see native flora and wildlife, making it an educational experience for kids.

- **Findeln Village:** The trek goes to Findeln, a charming village with typical wooden chalets. There are various mountain restaurants where you may try native Swiss cuisine.

Tips
- **Family-Friendly Amenities:** Sunnegga and Findeln have family-friendly amenities, such as picnic areas and playgrounds.
- **Stroller Accessible:** The walk is largely level and broad, making it suitable for strollers.
- **Water and Snacks:** Bring water and snacks, particularly to enjoy a picnic at Leisee.

Moos Trail: Nature Exploration for Kids

The Moos-Trail is intended for youngsters and provides an instructive nature exploring experience. This route includes interactive stations and is ideal for a fun family outing.

Route Details
- **Starting Point:** Furi (accessible by cable car from Zermatt).
- **Distance:** About 2 kilometers (1.2 miles).
- **Elevation Gain:** Minimal
- **Difficulty:** Easy
- **Duration:** 1–2 hours

Highlights
- **Interactive Stations:** The Moos-Trail offers educational and entertaining activities for youngsters. These stations provide information about local animals, flora, and the natural environment.

- **Furi Suspension Bridge:** The Furi suspension bridge highlights this path, providing an exciting trek over a steep valley. This is a beloved area for both youngsters and adults.

- **Alpine Environment:** The track winds through picturesque alpine meadows and woodlands, providing an opportunity to see animals such as marmots and birds.

- **Educational Experience:** The path is intended to be both enjoyable and informative, with information boards and interactive features that educate youngsters about the natural world.

Tips
- **Comfortable Footwear:** Children should wear comfortable walking shoes or boots appropriate for difficult terrain.
- **Supervision:** Always monitor minors, particularly when they cross the suspension bridge.
- **Picnic Area:** Bring a picnic and enjoy it at one of the authorized areas along the path.

Wolli Adventure Park: Fun for All Ages

Wolli Adventure Park in Sunnegga offers an adventure playground for children of all ages. It provides a range of activities and attractions, making it an ideal family vacation.

Route Details
- **Location:** Sunnegga (by funicular from Zermatt)
- **Activities:** Adventure and play areas
- **Duration:** Half-day to full-day visit.

Highlights
- **Adventure Playground:** Wolli Adventure Park offers a large adventure playground with climbing platforms, swings, slides, and more. It is intended to amuse children of all ages.

- **Leisee Lake:** The park is situated near Leisee Lake, where families may swim, paddle, and play water activities. There are also BBQ spots for family gatherings.

- **Teaching Elements:** The park has teaching stations where children may learn about the alpine environment, local species, and the value of conservation.

- **Hiking Routes:** Several family-friendly hiking routes begin near Sunnegga, enabling families to combine a trip to the adventure park with a lovely trek.

- **Mountain Restaurants:** There are various restaurants around where families may eat and drink.

Tips
- **Swimsuit:** Bring swimsuits and towels to enjoy the lake.
- **Sun Protection:** Because the park is located at a high altitude, use sunscreen and hats to protect yourself from the sun.
- **Adventure Kit:** Pack an adventure kit for youngsters that includes a magnifying glass, binoculars, and a tiny notepad to record environmental observations.

General Tips for Family Hikes in Zermatt

1. Plan Ahead: Before going out, check the weather forecast and trail conditions. Choose paths appropriate for your family's fitness level and interests.
2. Begin Early: Hike early in the day to avoid crowds and enjoy cooler weather.

3. Stay Hydrated: Bring plenty of water for everyone and take frequent pauses to relax and rehydrate.

4. Layer Up: Dress in layers to accommodate changing weather conditions. High-altitude weather may be unexpected, so it's best to prepare.

5. Safety First: Always stay on defined routes and keep a watch on youngsters, particularly in locations with steep drops or near water.

6. Leave No Trace: Teach youngsters about the principles of Leave No Trace to help maintain the natural beauty of the environment. Encourage kids to clean up rubbish and respect animals and vegetation.

7. Engage Kids: Keep children's attention by pointing out intriguing flora, animals, and geological characteristics. Make the trek an enjoyable and instructive experience.

These family-friendly hikes in Zermatt combine adventure, education, and natural beauty to provide an unforgettable experience for the whole family.

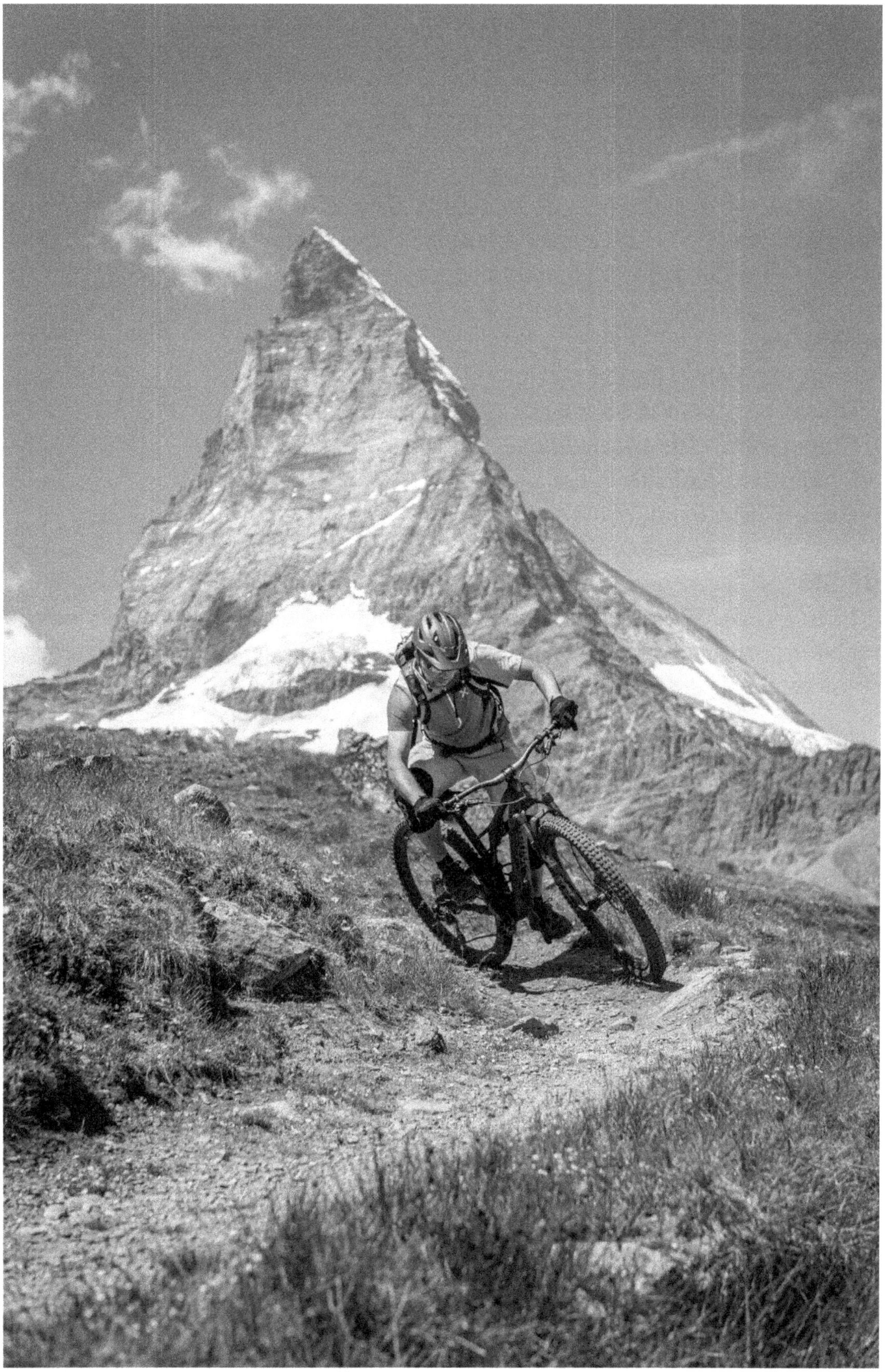

Advanced Hiking Routes in Zermatt

Hohbalmen: Challenging and Rewarding

The Hohbalmen trek is a hard but rewarding walk with stunning panoramic views in Zermatt. This track is ideal for experienced hikers seeking a challenging walk with considerable elevation gain and breathtaking vistas.

Route Details
- **Starting Point:** Zermatt town center
- **Distance:** About 18 kilometers (11.2 miles) round trip
- **Elevation Gain:** Approximately 1,300 meters (4,265 ft).
- **Difficulty:** Difficult.
- **Duration:** 7–9 hours

Highlights
- **Panoramic Views:** The Hohbalmen ridge provides panoramic views of the Matterhorn, Weisshorn, Zinalrothorn, and Dent Blanche. The 360-degree vista is among the most stunning in the Alps.

- **Flora & Fauna:** The route winds through rich alpine meadows, where you may see a variety of wildflowers and fauna, such as marmots and ibex.

- **Edelweiss Gardens:** As you rise, you'll come across places abundant with Edelweiss, the iconic alpine flower.

- **Remote Wilderness:** The track leads you to more isolated and less-frequented locations, creating a feeling of seclusion and connection with nature.

Route Description
- **Starting Out:** Begin your walk from Zermatt and go towards the Trift Valley. The first leg is a gradual ascent through the woodlands and past waterfalls.

- **Trift and Edelweiss Gardens:** Continue up to the Trift Hotel, an ancient mountain hotel, before heading to the Edelweiss Gardens. This portion is steep and difficult, but it gives wonderful vistas.

- **Hohbalmen Ridge:** The last push to the Hohbalmen Ridge is the most difficult section of the climb, but it is rewarded with breathtaking panoramic vistas.

Descent: After taking in the sights, return along the same road or take a different way down the Zmutt valley for a variety of scenery.

Tips
- **Start Early:** Start early to avoid afternoon thunderstorms and allow enough time to finish the course.
- **Hydration and Nutrition:** Bring lots of water and high-energy foods to keep you going during the lengthy journey.
- **Navigation:** While the track is well-marked, bringing a map or GPS gadget is suggested for added safety.
- **Weather Awareness:** Before leaving, check the weather prediction, since circumstances may change quickly in the mountains.

Breithorn Ascent: High-Altitude Adventure

Climbing the Breithorn is a high-altitude activity that provides a taste of alpine climbing without needing advanced technical abilities. Standing at 4,164 meters (13,661 feet), the Breithorn is one of the most accessible 4,000-meter summits in the Alps, making it a popular option for experienced hikers eager to test their boundaries.

Route Details
- **Starting Point:** Start at Klein Matterhorn (by cable car from Zermatt).
- **Distance:** About 6 kilometers (3.7 miles) round trip.
- **Elevation Gain:** Approximately 700 meters (2,297 ft).
- **Difficulty:** Difficult (because of elevation and glacier travel)
- **Duration:** 4-5 hours.

Highlights
- **Summit Views:** Breithorn Top offers stunning views of the Matterhorn, Mont Blanc, and the Bernese Alps.

- **Glacier Crossing:** The path crosses the Breithorn Plateau, a massive glacier that offers a fascinating and hard trekking experience.

- **High-Altitude Experience:** Climbing to almost 4,000 meters provides a truly high-altitude journey, replete with thin air and panoramic panoramas reminiscent of the Alps.

Route Description
- **Starting Out:** Begin by taking the cable car from Zermatt to Klein Matterhorn. The cable car trip alone provides breathtaking vistas and is an experience in its own right.

- **Glacier Crossing:** The path begins at Klein Matterhorn and continues over the Breithorn Plateau. This segment contains glacier travel, therefore crampons and an ice axe are required, and rope usage is advised.

- **Ascent:** The final ascent to the Breithorn top is a steady climb on snow and ice. The grade is mild but constant.

- **Summit:** Climb to the peak and take in the wonderful views before descending using the same path.

Tips
- **Guided Ascent:** For those unfamiliar with glacier trekking or high-altitude mountaineering, consider hiring a mountain guide.
- **Acclimatization:** To lessen the danger of altitude sickness, spend a few days acclimatizing in Zermatt or at high elevations before trying the trip.
- **Required Equipment:** Wear crampons, carry an ice axe, and utilize ropes as needed. Make sure you have appropriate attire for the cold, windy weather at high elevations.
- **Physical Preparation:** Be in excellent physical shape and familiar with intense exertion at high heights.

Hörnli Hut: Near the Matterhorn

The walk to the Hörnli Hut on the Matterhorn is a hard and iconic path that puts you close to one of the world's most recognized mountains. The hut is the starting point for climbers tackling the Matterhorn, although the walk itself is rewarding for experienced hikers.

Route Details
- **Starting Point:** Start in Schwarzsee, accessible by cable car from Zermatt.
- **Distance:** About 8 kilometers (5 miles) round trip.
- **Elevation Gain:** Around 850 meters (2,789 feet).
- **Difficulty:** Difficult.
- **Duration:** 4-5 hours.

Highlights
- **Matterhorn View:** The hike provides breathtaking views of the Matterhorn's north face.

- **Historical Hut:** The Hörnli Hut has a rich climbing history and has long served as the customary base camp for Matterhorn climbers.

- **Alpine Terrain:** The trek takes you through a variety of alpine terrain, including rocky trails, scree slopes, and snowfields, for a truly high-mountain experience.

- **Wildlife:** Look for ibex, chamois, and marmots along the route.

Route Description
- **Starting Out:** Begin the walk at Schwarzsee, a lovely lake with reflections of Matterhorn. The first segment follows a well-marked trail across alpine meadows.

- **Ascent:** As you approach the hut, the terrain gets steeper and more rough. The last stage includes climbing over boulders and traversing snowfields.

- **Hörnli Hut:** Climb to the Hörnli Hut (3,260 meters or 10,696 ft) for breathtaking views of the Matterhorn and its neighboring peaks. The hut serves refreshments and is an excellent location to relax and take in the surroundings.

- **Descend:** Follow the same path back to Schwarzsee, taking care of the steep and rocky areas.

Tips
- **Early Start:** Start early to avoid afternoon storms and have enough daylight for your walk.
- **Physical Fitness:** You must be in great physical shape for the trek, which is demanding and entails substantial elevation gain.
- **Scrambling Skills:** Be familiar with scrambling and exposed terrain. Some parts of the route need the use of hands for balance and stability.
- **Weather Preparation:** Check the weather forecast and be ready for unforeseen changes. Carry adequate gear for cold and windy weather.

General Tips for Advanced Hiking in Zermatt

1. Essential Gear: Always include a map, compass, or GPS, first aid kit, extra food and water, a headlamp, and layers of clothes.

2. Navigation: Make sure you are acquainted with the route and possess the appropriate navigation abilities. Advanced paths may have fewer frequent markers.

3. Acclimatization: To reduce the risk of altitude sickness, acclimate at high elevations before trying difficult excursions.

4. Emergency Preparedness: Locate the closest emergency services and carry a cell phone or communication device.

5. Physical Training: Regular cardiovascular and strength training can help you improve the endurance and muscular strength you'll need for tough treks.

6. Respect Nature: Use Leave No Trace principles to maintain the paths' natural beauty while also protecting the ecosystem.

7. Hiking Partners: To ensure safety, hike with a companion or group whenever feasible, particularly on isolated and difficult paths.

These tough hiking paths in Zermatt combine hard climbs, high-altitude obstacles, and exceptional visual rewards. Whether you're summiting a 4,000-meter mountain, trekking glaciers, or climbing across steep slopes, these climbs provide remarkable experiences for seasoned explorers.

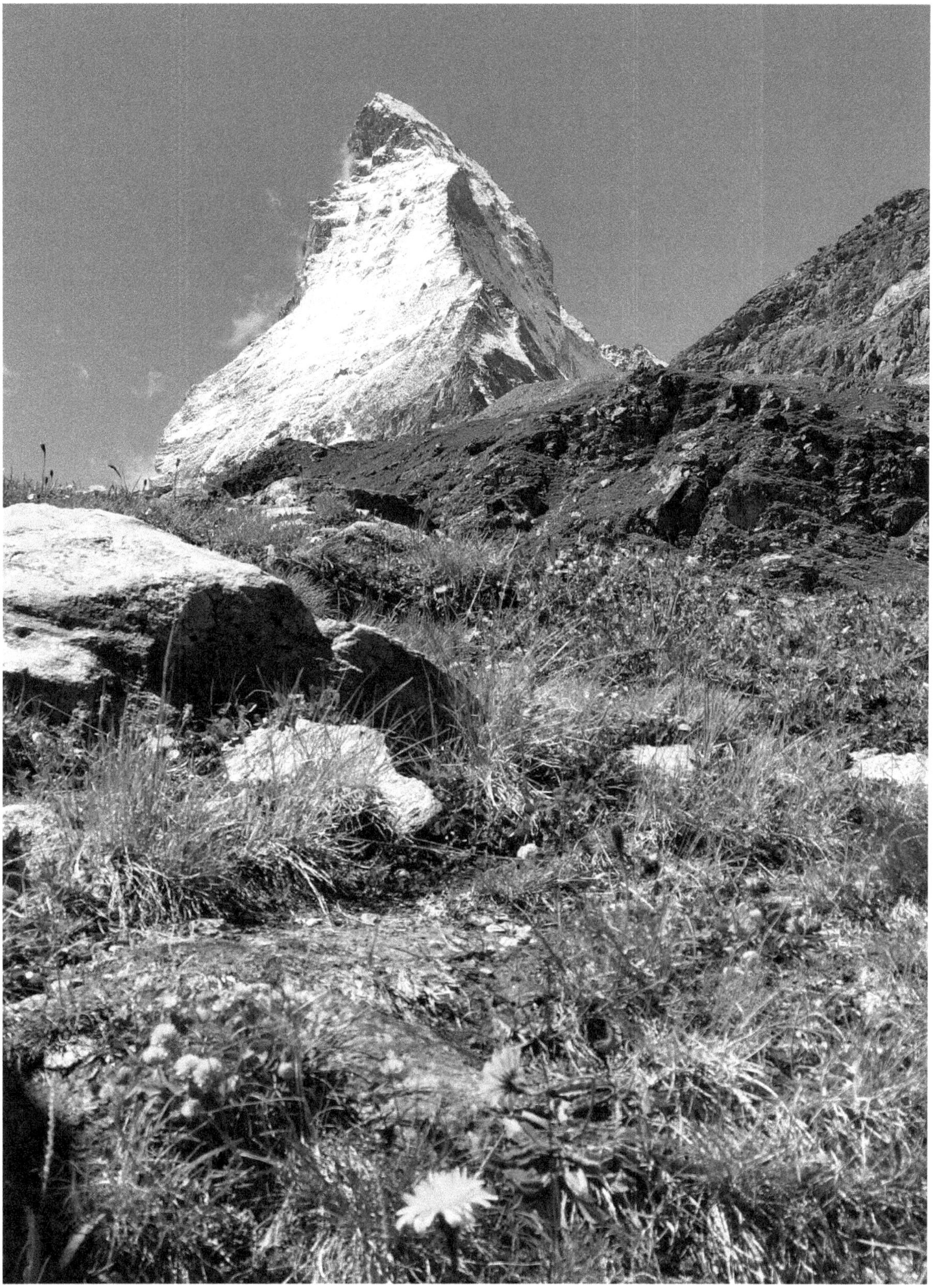

Multi-Day Hiking Adventures in Zermatt

The Haute Route: Zermatt to Chamonix

The Haute Route is a well-known long-distance trek that connects Zermatt, Switzerland, and Chamonix, France. This multi-day walk takes you into the heart of the Swiss Alps, via breathtaking mountain scenery, secluded valleys, and high alpine passes. It provides a mix of hard terrain, gorgeous views, and a rich cultural experience.

Route Details
- **Starting Point:** Zermatt, Switzerland.
- **Endpoint:** Chamonix, France.
- **Distance:** About 180 kilometers (112 miles).
- **Elevation Gain:** Variable, with substantial ascents and descents.
- **Duration:** 10–14 days
- **Difficulty:** Difficult.

Highlights
- **Panoramic Views:** Panoramic views of prominent peaks such as Matterhorn, Mont Blanc, and Dent Blanche.

- **High Alpine Passes:** Pass through numerous high passes, including the Col de Prafleuri, Col des Roux, and Col de la Chaux, each of which has its own set of obstacles and rewards.

- **Glaciers and Snowfields:** Travel through beautiful glaciers and snowfields for a truly high-mountain experience.

- **Mountain Huts and Communities:** Stay in classic mountain huts and picturesque alpine communities to experience local friendliness and culture.

- **Wildlife and Flora:** See a variety of species, including ibex, chamois, and marmots, as well as the lush alpine vegetation.

Route Description
Day 1
- **Zermatt to Zinal:** The trek starts in Zermatt with a tough climb to the Col de Tracuit. Enjoy panoramic views of the Matterhorn and its neighboring peaks. Overnight at the mountain town of Zinal.

Day 2-4
- **Zinal to Arolla:** Travel through gorgeous valleys and over high passes such as the Col de Torrent and Col de Reidmatten. Stay in mountain cottages or small settlements along the road.

Day 5-7
- **Arolla to Verbier:** From Arolla to Verbier Cross difficult passes like the Col de Louvie and Col de Prafleuri while traversing glaciers and rough terrain. Verbier provides a pleasant stay with facilities.

Day 8-10
- **Verbier to Champex-Lac:** Take picturesque paths through alpine meadows and woodlands, passing past the stunning Lacs des Dix and Mauvoisin.

Day 11-14
- **Champex-Lac to Chamonix:** The last part involves the strenuous climb of the Col de Balme, which provides breathtaking vistas of Mont Blanc. Descend into the Chamonix Valley to complete your adventure in this famous climbing center.

Tips
- **Preparation:** Physical preparation is crucial for the long and challenging hike. Regular cardiovascular and strength exercise is suggested.
- **Gear:** Bring a robust backpack, high-quality hiking boots, weather-resistant clothes, a sleeping bag, and navigation instruments.
- **Guided Tours:** If you're new to alpine hiking, consider taking a guided trip. Guides provide experience, safety, and logistical help.
- **Permits & Bookings:** Check for any necessary permits and make bookings for mountain lodges in advance, particularly during peak hiking season.

Tour of Monte Rosa: Epic Mountain Journey

The Tour of Monte Rosa is a multi-day walk that circumnavigates the Monte Rosa range, the Alps' second-highest peak. This route provides a tough and rewarding experience by combining rough terrain, high passes, and stunning views. The route takes you through Swiss and Italian territory, delivering a unique cultural experience.

Route Details
- **Starting Point:** Zermatt, Switzerland.
- **End Point:** Zermatt, Switzerland (round path)
- **Distance:** About 160 kilometers (99 miles).
- **Elevation Gain:** Major ascents and descents
- **Duration:** 9 to 12 days.
- **Difficulty:** Difficult.

Highlights
- **Monte Rosa Massif:** Explore the magnificence of the Monte Rosa Massif, with towering peaks and vast glaciers.

- **Diverse Landscapes:** The path travels through alpine meadows, rugged peaks, lush valleys, and high-altitude passes.

- **Cultural Experience:** The walk crosses the Swiss-Italian border many times, giving you a chance to sample both nations' diverse cultures, cuisines, and languages.

- **Historic Routes:** Travel over old trade routes and pathways utilized by mountaineers for generations.

- **Mountain Refuges:** Stay in traditional mountain refuges and huts, enjoying the company of other hikers and the kindness of the owners.

Route Description
Day 1
- **Zermatt to Theodul Pass:** Begin in Zermatt with a tough climb to Theodul Pass, offering breathtaking views of the Matterhorn. Overnight at Rifugio Teodulo.

Day 2-4
- **Theodul Pass to Gressoney-La-Trinité:** Cross high passes such as the Colle di Bettaforca and Colle del Lys, passing through glaciers and snowfields. Descend to the lovely Italian valley of Gressoney.

Day 5-7
- **Gressoney-La-Trinité to Macugnaga:** Cross the Passo dei Salati and take in the stunning vistas of the Anzasca valley. Macugnaga, a lovely Italian town, provides a relaxing stay.

Day 8-10
- **Macugnaga to Saas-Fee:** Continue through rugged alpine terrain and cross the Monte Moro Pass back into Switzerland. Saas-Fee is a picturesque, car-free community recognized for its alpine beauty.

Days 11 and 12
- **Saas-Fee to Zermatt:** The last stage involves a climb of the Passo del Monte Moro and a return to Zermatt, completing the round path around Monte Rosa.

Tips
- **Altitude Acclimatization:** To reduce the danger of altitude sickness, spend a few days acclimatizing at high-altitude places like Zermatt before embarking on the climb.
- **Navigation Abilities:** The path may be difficult to traverse, so make sure you have decent map reading abilities or a dependable GPS device.

- **Fitness Level:** The journey consists of lengthy days with major elevation changes, so you should be in great physical shape.
- **Weather Preparation:** Be prepared for quickly changing weather conditions, particularly at higher elevations. Carry the necessary gear for cold, damp, and windy conditions.

Walker's Haute Route: Stunning Landscapes.

The Walker's Haute Route is a popular multi-day walk from Chamonix, France to Zermatt, Switzerland. This route is known for its breathtaking beauty, which includes spectacular mountain vistas, attractive alpine communities, and lush valleys. Unlike the conventional Haute Route, which includes glacier travel, the Walker's Haute Route follows high mountain paths, making it more accessible to experienced hikers who need climbing expertise.

Route Details
- **Starting point:** Chamonix, France.
- **End Point:** Zermatt, Switzerland
- **Distance:** About 200 kilometers (124 miles).
- **Elevation Gain:** Significant ascents and descents.
- **Duration:** 12 to 14 days
- **Difficulty:** Difficult.

Highlights
- **Iconic Peaks:** Experience stunning views of legendary peaks including Mont Blanc, Grand Combin, and Matterhorn.

- **Diverse Terrain:** The route travels through high mountain passes, steep hills, verdant valleys, and attractive towns.

- **Cultural Immersion:** Discover the distinct combination of French and Swiss alpine culture, food, and hospitality.

- **Remote Wilderness:** Hike into distant, unspoiled wilderness regions for a feeling of isolation and adventure.

- **Mountain Refuges:** Stay in well-equipped mountain refuges and alpine cabins while enjoying the company of other hikers.

Route Description

Day 1
- **Chamonix to Argentière:** Begin in Chamonix with a magnificent stroll through lush woods and alpine meadows.

Day 2-4
- **Argentière to Champex-Lac:** Cross high passes like the Col de Balme and the Col de Forclaz, taking in the breathtaking scenery and diverse terrain. Champex-Lac is a beautiful lakeside town.

Day 5-7
- **Champex-Lac to Arolla:** Travel through picturesque valleys and over high passes such as the Fenêtre d'Arpette and Col de Prafleuri. Arolla is a picturesque mountain town.

Day 8-10
- **Arolla to Zinal:** Travel through isolated and difficult terrain, traversing passes like the Col des Roux and Col de Tsate. Enjoy the mountain landscape while staying in historic cabins.

Days 11-12
- **Zinal to Gruben:** The course continues through breathtaking scenery, with hard ascents and descents. Gruben is a tiny and remote settlement.

Day 13-14
- **Gruben to Zermatt:** The last stage involves the climb of the Augstbordpass and a descent into the Mattertal valley, with the journey ending in Zermatt.

Tips
- **Physical Preparation:** The walk requires exceptional physical condition due to lengthy days, large elevation changes, and hard terrain.
- **Navigation Tools:** Bring precise maps, a GPS device, and a guidebook to help you navigate the journey properly.
- **Weather Awareness:** Be prepared for changing weather conditions and have suitable attire for rain, wind, and frigid temperatures.
- **Resupply Locations:** Designate restock locations for food and other necessities along the trip. Some settlements and shelters provide groceries and meals.
- **Water and Nourishment:** Make sure you have enough water and nourishment, particularly during the more distant stages of the walk. Carry water purification pills or a filter to ensure safe drinking water from natural sources.

General Tips for Multi-Day Hiking Adventures

1. Physical Conditioning: Regular cardiovascular and strength training can help you prepare for the physical demands of multi-day hikes. Work on endurance and leg strength.

2. Quality Gear: Invest in a sturdy backpack, comfortable and supportive hiking boots, moisture-wicking apparel, and a dependable sleeping bag.

3. Navigation Skills: Learn how to read maps, use a compass, and navigate using GPS. Bring comprehensive maps and a guidebook tailored to the journey.

4. Packing Light: Pack effectively and just bring what you need to make your bag as light as possible. Prioritize lightweight, multipurpose gear.

5. Hydration and Nutrition: To stay hydrated, drink lots of water and eat high-energy snacks. Plan your meals wisely and pick light, high-calorie alternatives.

6. Weather Preparedness: Be prepared for quickly changing weather conditions, particularly in high-alpine locations. Pack layers to adapt to temperature changes.

7. Emergency Preparedness: Bring a first-aid kit, a whistle, a torch or headlamp, and an emergency shelter. Understand the location of the closest emergency services and carry a communication device.

8. Acclimatization: To lessen the risk of altitude sickness, spend a few days acclimating at higher elevations before beginning your climb.

9. Respect the Environment: To reduce your environmental effects, use the Leave No Trace guidelines. Take out all rubbish and respect the local animals and flowers.

10. Permits and Rules: Check for any route-specific permits or rules and make the appropriate preparations ahead of time.

Zermatt and its surroundings provide some of the most stunning and rewarding multi-day trekking experiences in the world. Whether you're traveling high alpine passes on the Haute Route, circumnavigating the spectacular Monte Rosa massif, or experiencing the many landscapes of the Walker's Haute Route, these treks provide unrivaled opportunities to experience the Swiss Alps' beauty and challenges. Proper planning, physical training, and respect for the natural environment will guarantee a safe and interesting journey. Enjoy the drive and the beautiful views that greet you at every bend.

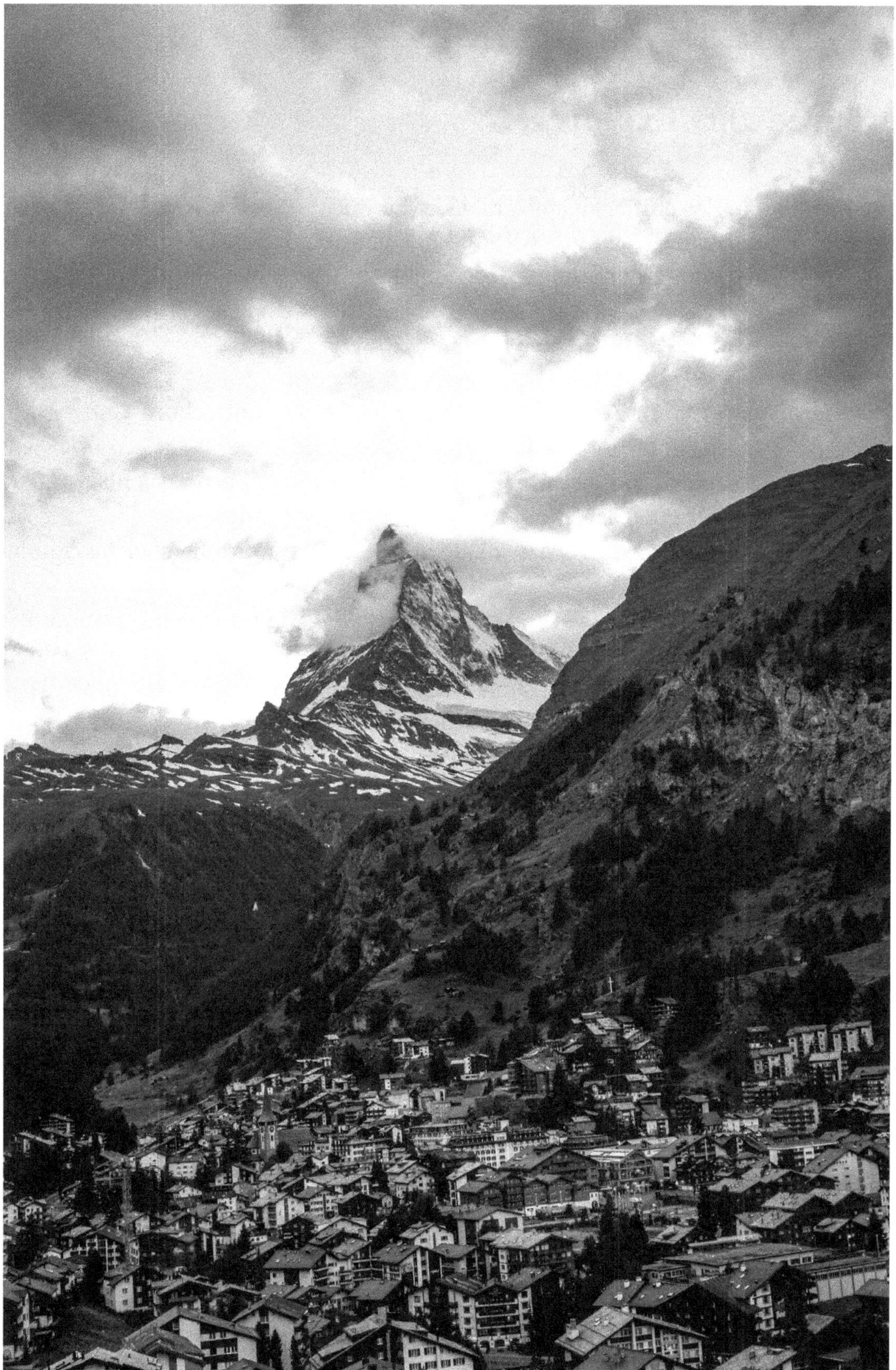

Itinerary Suggestions for Zermatt

The Three-Day Explorer

A three-day plan in Zermatt is ideal for hikers who want to see some of the region's most renowned routes and attractions without staying too long. This schedule aims to combine natural beauty, mild physical exertion, and cultural encounters.

Day 1: Arrival and Initial Exploration

- **Morning:** Arrive in Zermatt by scenic train on the Matterhorn Gotthard Bahn. Check into your hotel and freshen up.
- **Mid-morning:** Begin with a leisurely walk around Zermatt Village. Visit the Zermatt Museum to learn about the local history and culture.
- **Lunch:** Have a classic Swiss meal at a local restaurant, such as fondue or raclette.
- **Afternoon:** Board the Gornergrat Bahn for Gornergrat. The 33-minute ride provides stunning views of the Matterhorn and its neighboring peaks. When you get to Gornergrat, take a short trek around the region to appreciate the panoramic views and stop by the Gornergrat Observatory.
- **Evening:** Return to Zermatt for supper. Try some of the local dishes and unwind at a nice restaurant.

Day 2: Scenic Hikes and Alpine Lakes

- **Morning:** Take the funicular to Sunnegga. From Sunnegga, take the Five Lakes Walk (5-Seenweg), an easy trek that passes through five gorgeous alpine lakes: Stellisee, Grindjisee, Grünsee, Moosjisee, and Leisee. Each lake has stunning views of the Matterhorn and is ideal for photography.
- **Lunch:** Bring a picnic lunch to eat by one of the lakes, or go back to Sunnegga for a meal at a mountain restaurant.
- **Afternoon:** Continue exploring the paths surrounding Sunnegga or ride the funicular back to Zermatt. Explore the lovely village of Findeln, which is noted for its classic wooden chalets and panoramic vistas.
- **Evening:** Return to Zermatt and have supper at a local restaurant. Consider relaxing with a spa or wellness treatment at your hotel.

Day 3: Iconic Matterhorn Views

- **Morning:** Take the Matterhorn Glacier Paradise cable car to Europe's highest cable car station, 3,883 meters (12,739 ft). Enjoy panoramic views of the Matterhorn and the neighboring peaks. Visit the Glacier Palace, an ice cave filled with sculptures and tunnels cut from the glacier.
- **Mid-morning:** Begin the climb to Schwarzsee, a stunning alpine lake with Matterhorn reflections. The climb is modest and provides breathtaking views of the surrounding environment.
- **Lunch:** Enjoy lunch at the Schwarzsee restaurant while admiring the peaceful mountain scenery.
- **Afternoon:** Hike back to Zermatt or take the cable car for a slower descent. Spend your last hours in Zermatt touring the town, shopping for souvenirs, or sipping a farewell cup of coffee with mountain views.
- **Evening:** Depart from Zermatt, concluding your three-day adventure in this mountain wonderland.

The Weeklong Adventurer

A week in Zermatt provides for a more thorough exploration of the area's numerous hiking paths and natural beauties. This program combines strenuous walks, picturesque routes, and cultural events to thoroughly immerse you in the alpine landscape.

Day 1: Arrival and Village Exploration

- **Morning:** Arrive in Zermatt and check into your accommodations.
- **Mid-morning:** Explore Zermatt village, stopping at the Zermatt Museum and the Matterhorn Museum to learn about the region's climbing heritage.
- **Lunch:** Dine at a local restaurant and sample traditional Swiss cuisine.
- **Afternoon:** Enjoy a leisurely trek to the adjacent hamlet of Zmutt. This medieval community provides beautiful scenery and a glimpse of traditional alpine living.
- **Evening:** return to Zermatt for supper and rest.

Day 2: Gornergrat Adventure

- **Morning:** Board the Gornergrat Bahn for Gornergrat. Explore the magnificent vistas and explore the Gornergrat Observatory.
- **Mid-morning:** Hike from Gornergrat to Riffelberg, a picturesque path with spectacular views of the Matterhorn and neighboring peaks.

- **Lunch:** Have lunch at Riffelberg, either at a mountain restaurant or with a packed picnic.
- **Afternoon:** Continue trekking from Riffelberg to Riffelalp, then catch the train back to Zermatt.
- **Evening:** Dinner in Zermatt followed by a leisurely evening walk around the town.

Day 3: High Altitude Adventure

- **Morning:** Take the cable car to the Matterhorn Glacier Paradise. Explore the Glacier Palace and appreciate the views from Europe's highest cable car station.
- **Mid-morning:** Begin the fairly tough walk to Schwarzsee, which offers stunning views.
- **Lunch:** At the restaurant on Schwarzsee.
- **Afternoon:** Hike or ride the cable car back to Zermatt.
- **Evening:** Unwind with a spa treatment or spend a peaceful evening at your hotel.

Day 4: Edelweissweg and Sunnegga

- **Morning:** Ride the funicular to Sunnegga and begin the Edelweissweg climb. This route is notable for its profusion of alpine flowers and breathtaking vistas.
- **Lunch:** Have a picnic lunch along the path.
- **Afternoon:** Return to Sunnegga and visit Wolli Adventure Park, a family-friendly destination with activities for all ages.
- **Evening:** Return to Zermatt for supper and an evening of leisure.

Day 5: Advanced Hiking Challenge

- **Morning:** Take the cable car to Furi and begin the strenuous climb to Hörnli Hut, the base camp for Matterhorn ascents.
- **Mid-Morning:** Enjoy the trek, which provides close-up views of the Matterhorn and needs a moderate degree of fitness.
- **Lunch:** Eat at Hörnli Hut.
- **Afternoon:** Return to Furi and take the cable car to Zermatt.
- **Evening:** Unwind and recharge with a great lunch in Zermatt.

Day 6: Cultural and Historical Exploration

- **Morning:** Visit the Randa Suspension Bridge, which is one of the Alps' longest pedestrian suspension bridges. The climb to the bridge provides breathtaking vistas and an unforgettable experience.
- **Mid-morning:** Explore the bridge and nearby trails.
- **Lunch:** Return to Zermatt for lunch.
- **Afternoon:** Join a guided tour of the traditional Swiss communities around Zermatt, learning about local traditions and history.
- **Evening:** Dinner in Zermatt, then a visit to a local bar or café to enjoy the village's nightlife.

Day 7: Relaxation and Departure

- **Morning:** Spend your last day resting in Zermatt. Enjoy a leisurely breakfast and a morning spa treatment, or take a nice stroll around the town.
- **Lunch:** Enjoy a goodbye meal at a lovely restaurant.
- **Afternoon:** Shop for gifts and enjoy one more trip to Zermatt.
- **Evening:** Depart Zermatt to conclude your week-long journey.

The three-day and week-long tours provide extensive and engaging experiences in Zermatt. Whether you're a short-term tourist wanting a taste of alpine splendor or an explorer searching for an immersive exploration, these itineraries include a variety of activities and attractions that showcase the best of Zermatt's geography, culture, and natural marvels. Each day is planned to blend physical exercise with leisure, delivering a rewarding and unforgettable trip to this breathtaking section of the Swiss Alps.

Guided Tours and Local Guides in Zermatt

Advantages of Hiring a Guide

1. Expertise and Knowledge: Hiring a local guide offers important skills and an understanding of the location. Guides know the trails, geography, and weather patterns, resulting in a safer and more enjoyable excursion. They may give insights into the area's history, geology, flora, and animals, which can help you understand and appreciate the landscape.

2. Safety: Safety is a top priority in high-altitude and harsh locations. Guides are educated to manage crises, negotiate tough terrain, and identify symptoms of altitude sickness. Their presence considerably decreases the likelihood of accidents and assures you are fully prepared for any unexpected obstacles.

3. Navigation: Navigating Zermatt's trails may be challenging due to their many intersections and various difficulty levels. A guide keeps you on track, avoids any diversions, and gets you to your destination quickly. This is especially critical for longer, multi-day walks, when becoming lost might have significant implications.

4. Customized Experience: Local guides may customize the hiking experience based on your preferences, fitness level, and interests. Whether you choose a difficult climb, a picturesque route, or an emphasis on local culture and history, a guide may design an itinerary that suits you.

5. Language Barrier: In a multilingual location like the Swiss Alps, language hurdles may be challenging. Local guides may help bridge this gap by easing contact with villagers, hut wardens, and other hikers, resulting in a smoother, more pleasurable journey.

6. Logistics and Permits: Guides coordinate permits, hut bookings, and transportation throughout the hike. This enables you to concentrate exclusively on the walk and enjoy it without the hassle of preparation and organizing.

7. Cultural Insights: Working with a local guide offers valuable cultural insights. They may expose you to local cultures, traditions, and food, which can enhance your whole experience and create lasting memories.

8. Environmental Awareness: Guides encourage appropriate and sustainable hiking techniques. They teach hikers about Leave No Trace principles and assist in reducing the environmental effect of your journey, ensuring that the Alps' pure beauty is conserved for future generations.

Recommended Local Guides

1. Zermatt Alpin Center
Address: Bahnhofstrasse 58, 3920 Zermatt, Switzerland
Zermatt Alpin Center provides a variety of guided hiking trips and climbing adventures. Their professional guides give excellent knowledge of the area, ensuring a safe and interesting journey. They provide both group and private trips, catering to a variety of skill levels and interests.

2. Zermatters
Address: Bahnhofstrasse 58, 3920 Zermatt, Switzerland
Zermatters is a popular guiding business in Zermatt that offers experienced guides for hiking, climbing, and outdoor sports. Their guides are well-trained and enthusiastic about the Alps, and they provide bespoke trips that showcase the region's natural splendor.

3. Matterhorn Ultraks
Address: Obere Mattenstrasse 25, 3920 Zermatt, Switzerland
Matterhorn Ultraks specializes in trail running and high-altitude climbing, offering experienced coaching for those seeking tough excursions. Their guides are experienced athletes who have extensive knowledge of the routes and terrain, assuring an exciting and safe trip.

4. Bergführer Zermatt
Address: Tuftra 1, 3920 Zermatt, Switzerland
Bergführer Zermatt provides individual guided trips led by experienced mountain guides. They specialize in high-altitude hikes, glacier treks, and challenging climbs, making them a good alternative for seasoned hikers seeking a more adventurous experience.

5. Alpine Exposure
Address: Obere Mattenstrasse 22, Zermatt 3920 Switzerland
Alpine Exposure offers guided hiking and photography experiences that combine the excitement of adventure with the skill of capturing breathtaking alpine scenery. Their guides are accomplished mountaineers and photographers, providing a unique and fascinating experience.

Booking Process

1. Research and Selection: Choose a guiding company that meets your requirements and interests. Consider the sort of trek, difficulty level, group size, and any unique interests you may have (for example, photography or history).

2. Contact the Company: Contact the chosen guiding agency through their website, email, or phone to ask about availability, particular trip specifics, and cost. Provide information about your hiking experience, fitness level, and any unique needs or preferences.

3. Reservation and Payment: Once the details have been verified, you may continue with the reservation. This usually entails filling out a booking form and paying a deposit or full payment. Some agencies may provide online booking systems for convenience.

4. Pre-journey Communication: Keep in contact with the guide agency in the weeks before your journey. They will supply you with necessary information, such as packing lists, meeting locations, and any further preparations required.

Hiring a local guide for your hiking journey in Zermatt has various advantages, ranging from increased safety and professional knowledge to a more customized and fulfilling experience. With so many renowned guiding firms to choose from, you're sure to discover the right guide for your tastes and ability level. By properly planning and budgeting, you may ensure a smooth and enjoyable hiking trip in the breathtaking Swiss Alps.

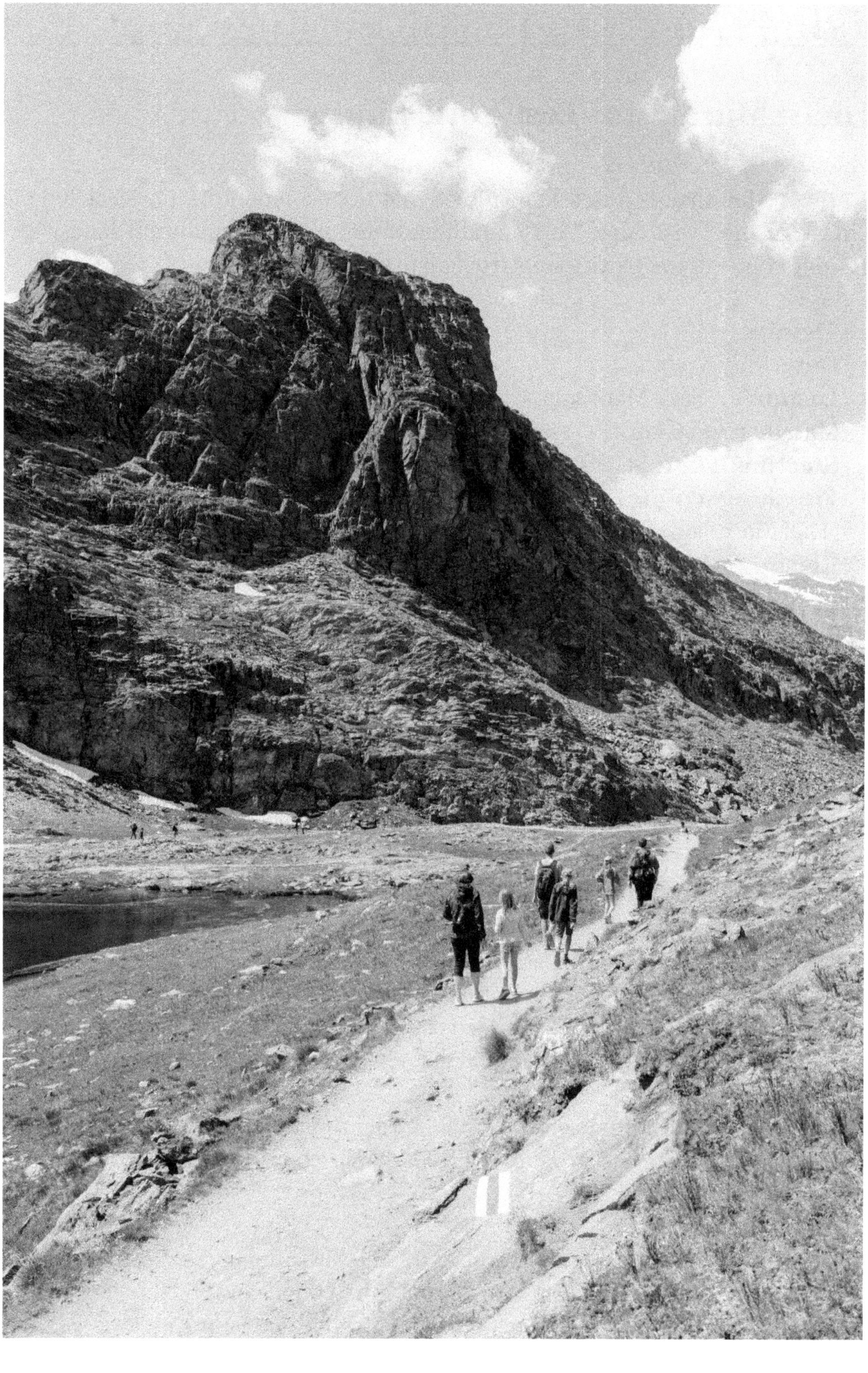

Hiking Events and Festivals in Zermatt 2024

Zermatt Marathon: Test Your Limits

The Zermatt Marathon is a well-known race that tests competitors' physical and mental endurance in the Swiss Alps. This marathon, noted for its magnificent landscape and challenging route, draws participants from all over the globe.

Event Details
- **Date:** July 6, 2024.
- **Distance:** Full Marathon (42.195 km), Half Marathon (21 km), and Ultra Marathon (45.6 km).
- **Starting Point:** St. Niklaus, Valais.
- **Finishing Points:** Riffelberg, Zermatt (Full and Ultra Marathon), Sunnegga (Half Marathon).
- **Elevation Gain:** About 1,940 meters during the whole marathon.

The Zermatt Marathon begins in the lovely village of St. Niklaus, in the Mattertal Valley. From there, racers go through lush woods, charming mountain communities, and picturesque pathways with breathtaking views of the surrounding peaks, including the legendary Matterhorn. The track steadily ascends, challenging the contestants' endurance and strength. The last stretch to Riffelberg is a difficult ascent that rewards with breathtaking views of the Swiss Alps.

Highlights
- **Scenic Beauty:** The marathon course offers breathtaking alpine vistas, including meadows, woods, and high-altitude paths.
- **Difficult Terrain:** The steep elevation rise and diverse terrain make this marathon a genuine test of endurance and fortitude.
- **Community Support:** The race is well-supported by local communities, with passionate spectators and volunteers cheering on the participants along the route.
- **Finish Line Experience:** Crossing the finish line at Riffelberg, with the Matterhorn in the background, is a remarkable experience for all competitors.

Tips for Participants
- **Training:** Proper training is crucial for the difficult course. Concentrate on hill running, endurance training, and adaptation to high elevations.
- **Gear:** Use trail running shoes and comfortable, moisture-wicking gear. Bring hydration packs, energy gels, and weather-appropriate clothing.

- **Acclimatization:** To lessen the risk of altitude sickness, spend a few days acclimatizing at Zermatt or another high-altitude region before the race.
- **Nutrition and Hydration:** Before and throughout the race, ensure that you eat and drink properly. Use aid stations along the way for refilling.
- **Pacing:** Begin at a comfortable speed to save energy for the difficult hills and final ascent.

The Gornergrat Nature Festival

The Gornergrat Nature Festival celebrates the natural beauty and ecological value of the Gornergrat region. This event combines hiking and educational activities to promote environmental awareness and conservation.

Event Details
- **Date:** June 21–23, 2024
- **Location:** Gornergrat and nearby trails.
- **Activities:** Guided nature walks, animal observation, informative presentations, and family-friendly events.

Highlights
- **Nature Treks:** Learn about the Gornergrat region's distinctive flora and animals during guided treks. Learn about the area's fauna, geology, and conservation activities.
- **Wildlife Observation:** Join guided wildlife observation sessions to witness marmots, ibex, and a variety of bird species.
- **Educational Talks:** Hear from experts on themes such as alpine ecosystems, climate change, and sustainable tourism.
- **Family Activities:** Engage in family-friendly activities including nature treasure hunts, interactive workshops, and storytelling sessions.

Tips for Participants
- **Family Participation:** The Festival is family-friendly, So bring your children to enjoy the festival's informative and engaging activities.
- **Gear:** Wear suitable hiking shoes and bring binoculars for animal viewing.
- **Environmental Awareness:** When hiking or participating in activities, adhere to the Leave No Trace principles and respect the natural environment.

Matterhorn Ultraks

This ultra-trail running event draws top runners and fans from across the globe. While it is largely geared at trail running, it also provides shorter distances and hiking choices, making it more accessible to a wider audience.

Event Details
- **Date:** August 23-25, 2024.
- **Location:** Zermatt and nearby trails.
- **Activities:** Ultra-trail races, short trail runs, guided walks, and family activities.

Highlights
- **Ultra-Trail Races:** Watching or participating in ultra-trail events, which test elite competitors' endurance and ability. The courses vary from 16 km to 49 km, with difficult terrain and substantial elevation gain.
- **Guided Treks:** Join guided treks on some of the most spectacular trails in the Zermatt area, providing a more relaxing approach to experience the event.
- **Family Events:** Participate in family-friendly activities and shorter trail runs intended specifically for children and novices.
- **Community Atmosphere:** The event develops a strong feeling of community by providing an opportunity for attendees to meet other outdoor enthusiasts and share their experiences.

Tips for Participants
- **Registration:** Early registration is recommended for races and guided walks, since seats may fill rapidly.
- **Training:** Get ready for the terrain and elevation gain of trail runs and treks. Training at higher elevations may be advantageous.
- **Gear:** Make sure you have proper trail running shoes and clothes. Bring necessities like water packs and energy gels.

Zermatt is a center for hiking and trail running events, providing a variety of challenges and experiences for outdoor lovers. Whether you're taking on the Zermatt Marathon or one of the numerous local hiking festivals, these events provide a one-of-a-kind chance to discover the breathtaking Swiss Alps. With adequate preparation, the correct gear, and a sense of adventure, you may fully appreciate the beauty and thrill of Zermatt's hiking events and festivals.

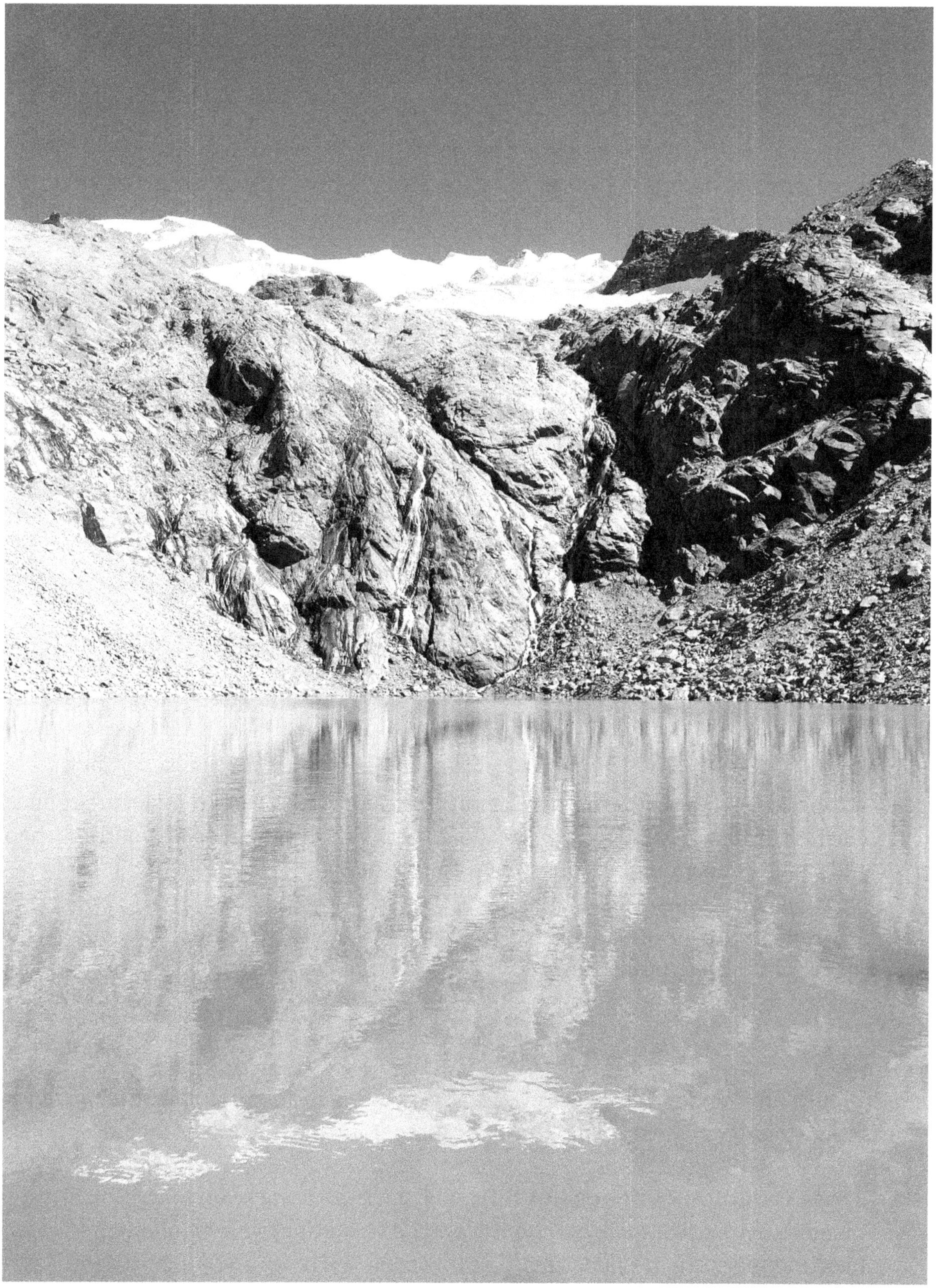

Flora and Fauna of the Swiss Alps

The Swiss Alps are known for their variety and distinct flora and fauna, which thrive in the severe but beautiful alpine climate. This ecosystem supports a diverse range of plant and animal species, many of which have evolved to live and thrive in high-altitude environments.

Alpine Flowers and Plants

1. Alpine Flowers
The Alpine area is known for its vivid flower displays throughout the short growing season. Some prominent alpine flowers you could find in the Swiss Alps are:

- **Edelweiss (Leontopodium alpinum):** The edelweiss, a symbol of rugged beauty, flourishes on rocky, high-altitude terrain. It features white star-shaped flowers and woolly leaves that protect it from cold weather.

- **Alpine Gentian (Gentiana alpina):** The alpine gentian, known for its brilliant blue blossoms, thrives in damp, calcareous soils at higher elevations. It flowers from midsummer to early fall, attracting pollinators including bees and butterflies.

- **Alpenrose (Rhododendron ferrugineum):** This evergreen shrub produces clusters of pink to crimson bell-shaped blooms. It grows on acidic, nutrient-poor soils and is often found in hilly areas of the Alps.

- **Alpine Aster (Aster alpinus):** This is a hardy perennial with daisy-like blooms in purple, pink, or white. It blooms from late spring to early summer and is often found in stony alpine meadows.

2. Alpine Plants
In addition to flowers, plants have evolved to flourish in tough alpine circumstances such as thin soils, strong winds, and dramatic temperature swings. This includes:

- **Moss Campion (Silene acaulis):** A cushion-forming plant with pink or white blooms that lives in rocky, exposed places. Its low, thick growth allows it to retain heat and moisture in colder areas.

- **Saxifrage (Saxifraga spp.):** These plants thrive in cracks and rocky slopes, producing tiny, star-shaped blooms in a variety of hues. They are designed to endure drought and rocky soil.

- **Alpine Grasses:** In alpine meadows, grass species such as Festuca spp. and Poa spp. create thick mats that provide food for grazing animals while also stabilizing soils.

Wildlife You Might Encounter

1. Ibex (Capra ibex): The ibex is a Swiss Alps icon, distinguished by its magnificent curving horns and nimble climbing ability. They like steep, rocky terrain and are often spotted grazing in alpine meadows.

2. Chamois (Rupicapra rupicapra): The chamois, which looks like an ibex but is smaller, is suited to rough terrain and may be found at higher elevations. It has small, hooked horns and is renowned for its agility and leaping skills.

3. Marmots (Marmota marmota): These huge ground-dwelling rodents are often seen in alpine meadows. They live in burrows and hibernate throughout the winter before emerging in the spring to seek for food.

4. Golden Eagle (Aquila chrysaetos): The golden eagle is a spectacular bird of prey that lives in the Swiss Alps. Its wingspan may reach 2.3 meters. It hunts small animals and birds, often flying high over hilly areas.

5. Ptarmigan (Lagopus muta): This bird is well-suited to alpine habitats, with plumage that varies from mottled brown in summer to pure white in winter, giving concealment against snow.

6. Alpine Salamander (Salamandra atra): The alpine salamander is an amphibian that lives in moist, cold places such as beneath rocks and in woods near water, despite the hard circumstances of the Swiss Alps.

Conservation and Responsible Hiking

1. Biodiversity Protection: The Swiss Alps support a diverse range of plant and animal species, many of which are protected by national and international conservation legislation. Habitat preservation, human impact reduction, and ecosystem restoration are the primary goals of conservation activities.

2. Leave No Trace Principles: Hikers are urged to adopt the Leave No Trace principles to reduce their environmental effects. This involves removing all litter, sticking to authorized pathways, respecting wildlife and vegetation, and not feeding or disturbing animals.

3. Trail Maintenance: To prevent destroying sensitive alpine plants, responsible hikers adhere to defined pathways. Trail maintenance staff aim to repair erosion, provide signs, and enhance the sustainability of major hiking trails.

4. Wildlife Protection: Hikers should watch animals from a safe distance, avoid approaching nests or dens, and abstain from feeding wildlife. This helps to preserve natural behaviors and decreases stress for animals.

5. Supporting Local Conservation Projects: Consider donating to local conservation groups and projects that seek to safeguard the Swiss Alps' natural heritage. Volunteering, giving, and engaging in educational programs are all options.

Exploring the Swiss Alps' flora and wildlife fosters a greater appreciation for the resilience and beauty of alpine ecosystems. From rare alpine flowers to famous animal species like ibex and golden eagles, each encounter enhances the trekking experience. Visitors may guarantee that future generations can enjoy and marvel at the marvels of the Swiss Alps by hiking responsibly and contributing to conservation initiatives.

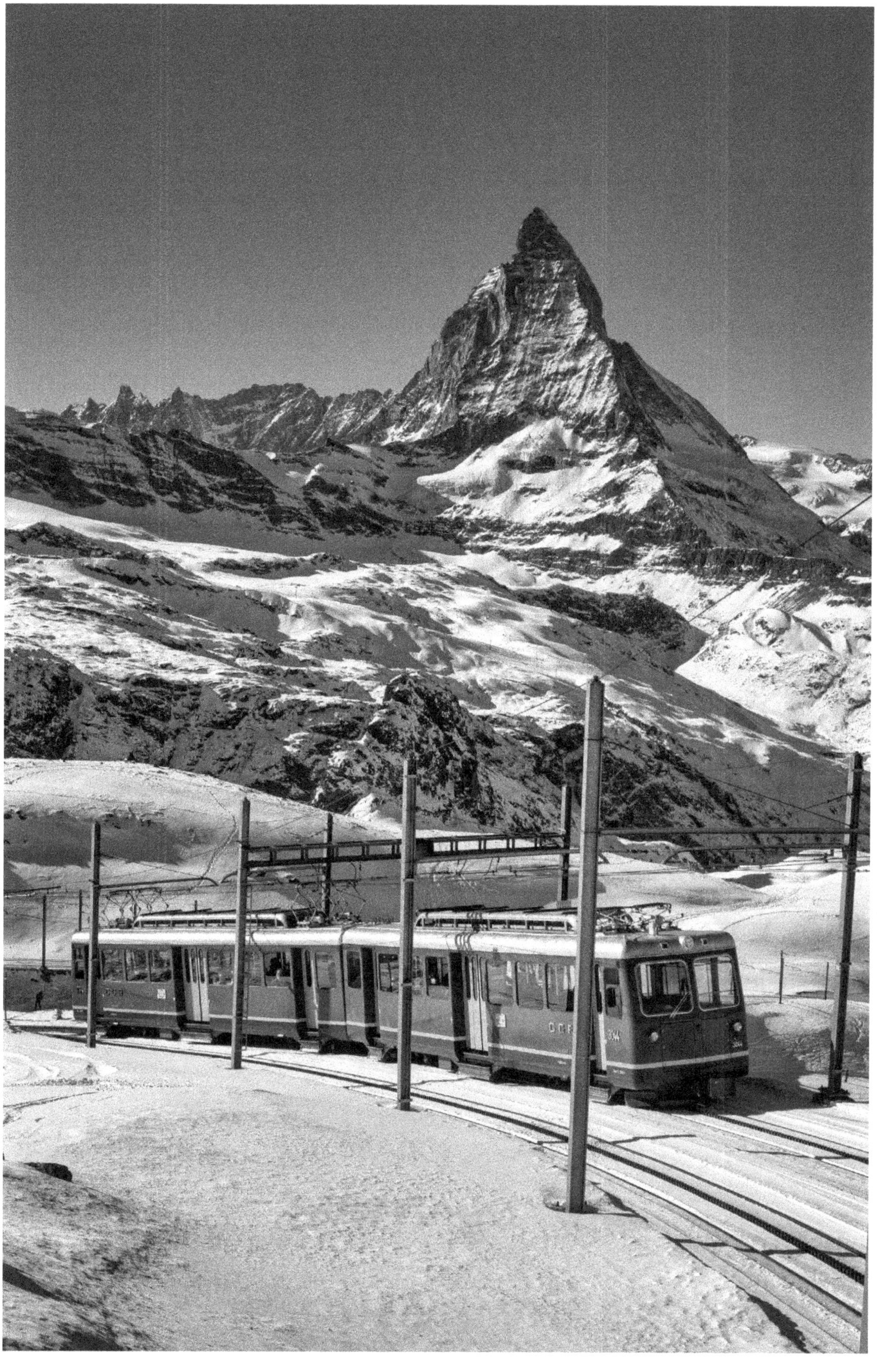

Cultural and Historical Highlights in Zermatt and the Swiss Alps

Traditional Swiss Villages

Switzerland is well-known for its charming communities hidden among the breathtaking Alpine vistas. These towns not only give natural beauty but also provide insight into Switzerland's rich cultural history and traditional way of life.

1. Zermatt: As the entryway to the famed Matterhorn and surrounded by some of the highest peaks in the Alps, Zermatt combines traditional Swiss charm with contemporary Alpine tourism. The town is car-free, keeping its picturesque character with tiny lanes lined with wooden chalets and colorful window shutters. Visitors may browse local artisan stores, bakeries selling Swiss specialties such as cakes and cheeses, and comfortable restaurants providing substantial Alpine cuisine.

2. Saas-Fee: Situated near Zermatt, Saas-Fee is another car-free community known for its well-preserved wooden buildings and barns. The community preserves its historic charm, with cobblestone streets, modest squares, and breathtaking views of the glaciers. Visitors may enjoy Swiss friendliness at family-owned hotels and restaurants that provide local delicacies.

3. Grindelwald: Nestled in the Bernese Alps, Grindelwald is a lovely resort famed for its alpine scenery and proximity to iconic peaks such as the Eiger. The community provides a variety of cultural activities, including traditional Swiss music performances and alpine festivals honoring local customs and traditions.

4. Lauterbrunnen: Nestled in a valley surrounded by towering cliffs and waterfalls, Lauterbrunnen is renowned for its natural beauty and classic Swiss architecture. Visitors may discover the Staubbach Falls, typical Swiss farms, and hiking routes that lead to panoramic views.

Zermatt Museum: Discover Local Heritage

1. Matterhorn Museum Zermatlantis: Located in Zermatt, this museum provides insight into the village's history and growth, as well as the trials and successes of climbing the Matterhorn. The exhibits contain relics, images, and interactive displays that highlight the history of climbing, local customs, and the influence of tourism on the area.

2. The Alpine Museum: The Swiss Alpine Museum, located in Bern, focuses on the Alps' cultural and ecological history. Multimedia presentations and temporary displays educate visitors about alpine flora and animals, traditional architecture, and mountain community life.

Historic Sites Along Hiking Trails

1. The Riffelsee: The Riffelsee, in Zermatt, is a glacier lake known for its beautiful reflection of the Matterhorn. It provides a calm setting to experience the natural splendor of the Alps and is just a short trek from the Gornergrat Railway station.

2. The Findel Glacier: This glacier in Zermatt exemplifies the region's geological history and provides chances for guided excursions to learn about glaciology and climate change.

3. The Gorner Canyon: Carved by the Gornera River, this canyon provides spectacular vistas of waterfalls, rock formations, and footbridges leading to breathtaking perspectives.

Exploring the cultural and historical attractions of Zermatt and the Swiss Alps provides a better appreciation of the region's rich history. From traditional Swiss towns and museums highlighting local history to historic locations along hiking routes revealing the geological and cultural importance of the Alps, each encounter immerses tourists in Switzerland's timeless beauty and culture. Whether you're admiring the Matterhorn from the Riffelsee, exploring the Matterhorn Museum Zermatlantis, or hiking through historic sites like the Gorner Gorge, these cultural and historical highlights add to the Swiss Alps' allure as a top destination for cultural exploration and outdoor adventure.

Après-Hiking in Zermatt

After a day of thrilling treks over the majestic Swiss Alps, Zermatt provides plenty of possibilities for relaxation, gastronomic pleasures, and rejuvenation to help you rest and recuperate from your outdoor experiences.

Best Places for Relaxation and Recovery

1. Gornergrat Restaurant & Shop: Situated at the summit of the Gornergrat Railway, this location provides panoramic views of the Matterhorn and neighboring peaks. Relax with a hot drink or a meal while taking in the beautiful views. It's the ideal location to relax after a long trek.

2. Kirchplatz: Zermatt's Center Plaza is a terrific location to relax and absorb the community ambiance. With its gorgeous church and old buildings, it's the perfect place for a leisurely walk or to relax and people-watch.

3. Sunnegga Paradise: This region provides breathtaking views of the Matterhorn and is accessible via funicular. It's a nice location to unwind by the Leisee Lake or have a picnic in a peaceful environment after your trek.

4. Zermatt's Cafés: Several cafés in Zermatt provide nice atmospheres in which to unwind with a cup of coffee or hot chocolate. Café Fuchs and Brown Cow Pub are popular places to relax and enjoy the local atmosphere.

Local Cuisine and Dining Recommendations

1. Swiss Chalet Food: Enjoy classic Swiss food in Zermatt's attractive eateries. Raclette, fondue, and rösti are must-try dishes.

- **Restaurant Schäferstube (Address: Riedstrasse 2, 3920 Zermatt, Switzerland):** Known for its traditional Swiss atmosphere and delectable lamb specialties. The rustic atmosphere and traditional food make it a popular option.

- **Restaurant Zum See (Address: Zum See 24, Zermatt 3920 Switzerland):** A short walk from Zermatt, this restaurant serves classic Swiss meals with a contemporary touch, accompanied by a comfortable mountain setting.

2. Fine Dining: Zermatt has numerous Michelin-starred restaurants for a more upmarket eating experience.

- **Restaurant Chez Vrony (Address: Findeln, 3920 Zermatt, Switzerland):** Chez Vrony, located on the Sunnegga slopes, is a family-run restaurant recognized for its rustic charm and superb cooking. It serves a distinct blend of classic Swiss cuisine and contemporary culinary inventions.

- **Findlerhof (Address:: Findeln, 3920 Zermatt, Switzerland):** Findlerhof is a lovely mountain eatery that has grown popular among residents and guests. It provides a superb dining experience centered on high-quality Swiss cuisine and spectacular vistas.

3. Casual Dining & Bars: Zermatt offers a range of relaxing dining options, including restaurants and bars.

- **Brown Cow Pub (Address: Bahnhofstrasse 41, 3920 Zermatt, Switzerland):** A favorite among hikers and skiers, it serves substantial pub meals in a calm setting.

- **Grampi's Bar and Restaurant (Address: Bahnhofstrasse 70, 3920 Zermatt, Switzerland):** With its vibrant environment and wide cuisine, it's an excellent place to relax with friends over a meal and beverages.

Wellness and Spa Options

1. The Spa at Mont Cervin Palace
Address: Bahnhofstrasse 31, 3920 Zermatt, Switzerland
The Spa at Mont Cervin Palace provides a variety of services, including massages, facials, and body treatments. The amenities include a sauna, steam bath, and heated indoor pool for a complete relaxing experience.

2. The Cervo Mountain Boutique Resort
Address: Riedweg 156, 3920 Zermatt, Switzerland
The Cervo Mountain Boutique Resort has an outdoor spa area with hot tubs, a Finnish sauna, and a relaxing area with breathtaking mountain views. It's an ideal place to relax after a day of trekking.

3. The Omnia
Address: Auf dem Fels, 3920 Zermatt, Switzerland
Known for its tranquil setting, The Omnia provides a spa with a sauna, Turkish bath, and an indoor/outdoor pool with stunning Matterhorn views. Wellness therapies emphasize holistic healing and relaxation.

4. The Riffelalp Resort
Address: 3920 Zermatt, Switzerland
Located at 2,222 meters above sea level, this resort provides a unique wellness experience with an outdoor pool, jacuzzi, and spa services. The magnificent vistas and tranquil surroundings add to the sensation of relaxation.

5. The Backstage Hotel Vernissage
Address: Hofmattstrasse 4, 3920 Zermatt, Switzerland
This hotel has a unique spa built by artist Heinz Julen. The spa experience consists of a sequence of treatments and baths themed on the seven days of creation, delivering a creative and refreshing experience.

Après-hiking in Zermatt combines leisure, gastronomic pleasures, and recuperation effortlessly. Whether you want to repose at breathtaking views like Gornergrat, eat traditional Swiss cuisine at local restaurants, or pamper yourself at elegant spas, Zermatt has many of alternatives to make your post-climb leisure as memorable as the trek itself. The village's pleasant ambiance, together with its numerous culinary and spa choices, make it the ideal place to rest and recharge before your next excursion in the breathtaking Swiss Alps.

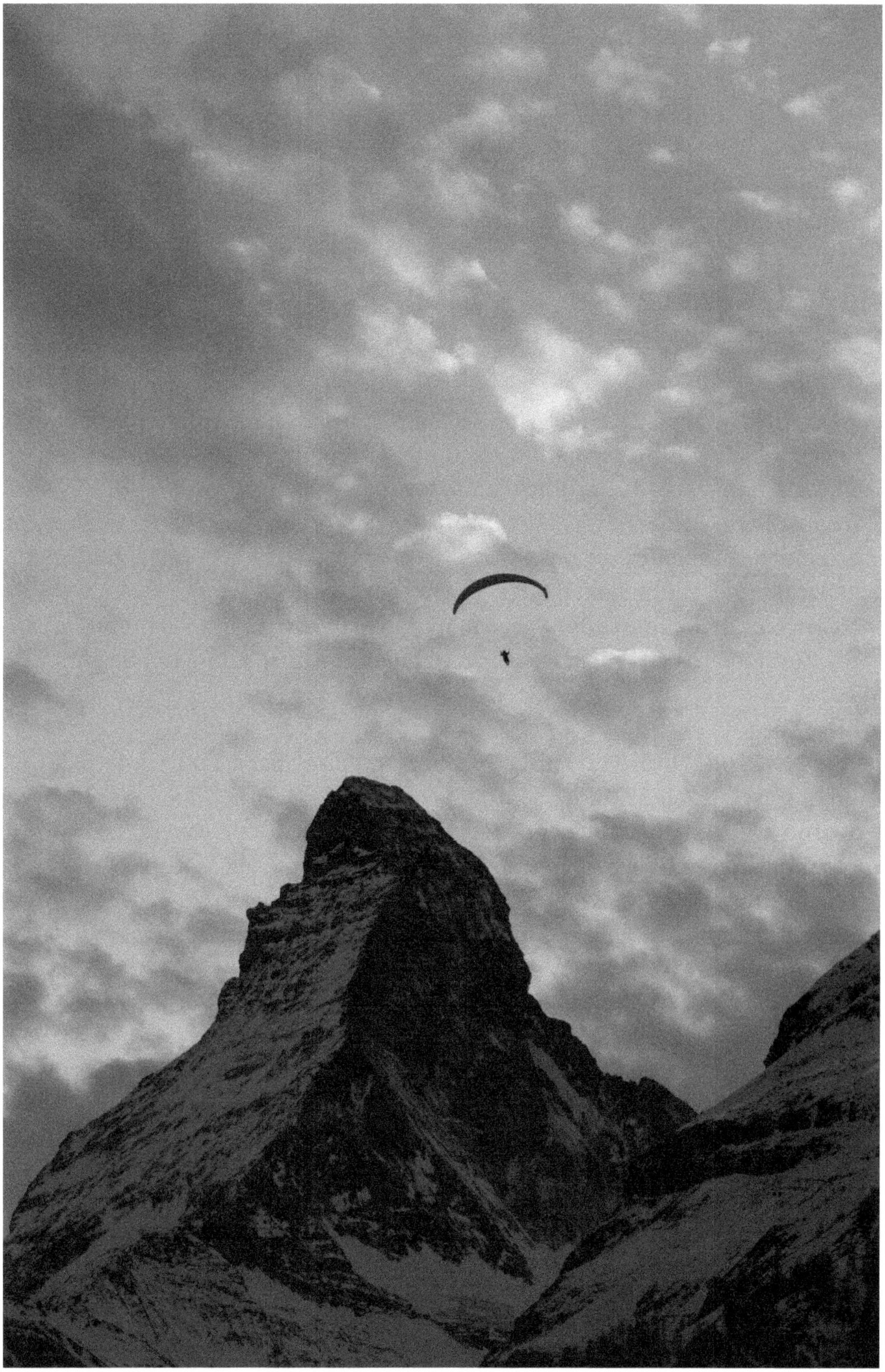

Practical Information for Hiking in Zermatt

When organizing a hiking vacation to Zermatt, it is essential to come prepared with practical knowledge to guarantee a safe and pleasurable experience. This complete reference includes maps and resources, emergency contacts and services, and helpful local language hints and phrases.

Maps & Resources

1. Trail Maps
- **Zermatt Tourist Office:** The Zermatt Tourist Office offers free hiking maps and booklets with information on routes, difficulty levels, and sites of interest. These are available at the office in the town center.
- **Swiss Topo Maps:** Swiss Topo provides comprehensive topographic maps that are indispensable for serious hikers. These maps include detailed information on geography, elevation, and paths.
- **Kompass Hiking Maps:** These maps, available both online and in shops, cover the Zermatt area and include clear route markers, distances, and heights.

2. Mobile Apps
- **SwitzerlandMobility:** This app offers precise maps and route planning for hiking, cycling, and outdoor sports. It contains GPS and offline maps.
- **Komoot:** This popular app for hikers and outdoor lovers provides route planning, navigation, and community-generated trail suggestions.
- **Maps.me:** An offline map app that downloads comprehensive maps of the Zermatt region, allowing you to navigate even when you don't have cell data.

Emergency Contacts and Services

1. Emergency Contacts
- **Swiss Emergency Number:** Switzerland's universal emergency number is 112. This will link you to the police, fire department, and medical services.
- **Mountain Rescue Service (REGA):** For mountain rescue operations, phone 1414. REGA conducts helicopter rescue services in the highlands.
- **Zermatt Emergency Number:** Call 144

2. Safety Tip
- **Weather Monitoring:** Check the weather prediction before hiking. Mountain weather may change quickly, so plan for unexpected fluctuations.
- **Path Conditions:** Be aware of path conditions, particularly if hiking early in the season when snow may still be present at higher elevations.
- **Buddy System:** If feasible, trek with a companion or group. If hiking alone, notify someone of your intended route and expected return time.

Local Language Tips and Phrases

Greetings and Basics

Hello: Hallo
Good morning: Guten Morgen
Good evening: Guten Abend
Goodbye: Auf Wiedersehen
Please: Bitte
Thank you: Danke
Yes: Ja
No: Nein
Excuse me/Sorry: Entschuldigung

Asking for Directions

Where is the trail to [place]? Wo ist der Weg nach [Ort]?
How far is it to [place]? Wie weit ist es nach [Ort]?
Is this the right way to [place]? Ist das der richtige Weg nach [Ort]?

Emergency Phrases

Help! Hilfe!
I need a doctor: Ich brauche einen Arzt.
Call the police: Rufen Sie die Polizei.
I am lost: Ich habe mich verirrt.
Can you help me? Können Sie mir helfen?

Dining and Accommodation

I would like to reserve a table: Ich möchte einen Tisch reservieren.
Can I see the menu, please? Kann ich bitte die Speisekarte sehen?

Do you have vegetarian options? Haben Sie vegetarische Gerichte?
I have a reservation: Ich habe eine Reservierung.
Is breakfast included? Ist das Frühstück inbegriffen?

Switzerland's four official languages are German, French, Italian, and Romansh. Zermatt's native language is Swiss German, however, many people also speak English. Here are some essential terms that can assist you manage your journey.

Equipping yourself with practical knowledge is essential for a safe and pleasurable hiking trip in Zermatt. Whether it's having the correct maps and resources, knowing the emergency contacts and services, or navigating with local language instructions, these elements make your vacation more enjoyable and guarantee you're prepared for anything. Being well-informed allows you to thoroughly immerse yourself in the beauty and culture of Zermatt and the Swiss Alps, making your hiking experience unforgettable and enjoyable.

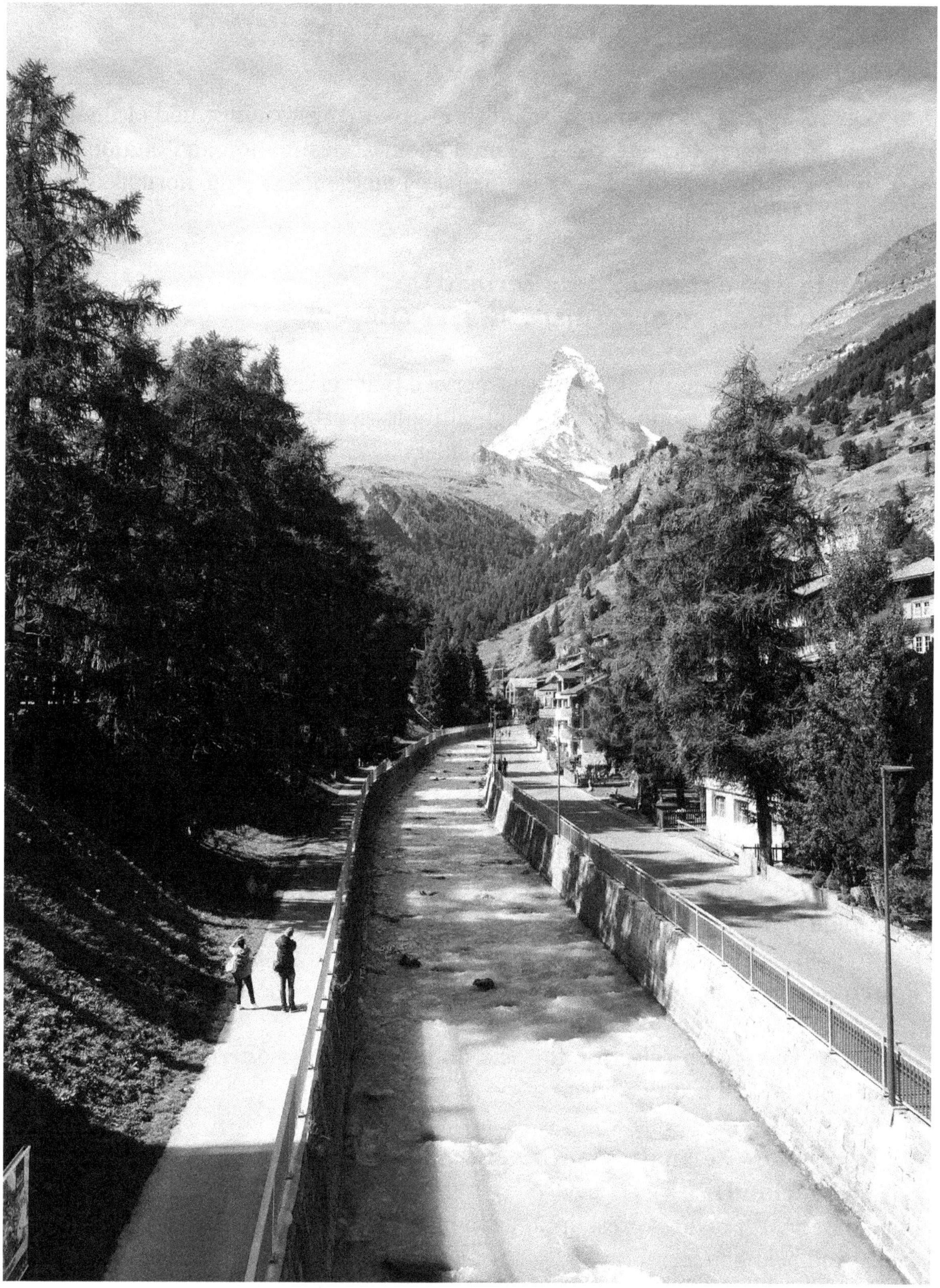

Medical Facilities in Zermatt

When organizing a hiking trip in Zermatt, it is essential to be informed of the medical services in the region. Zermatt, being a famous tourist destination and outdoor activity center, has enough medical services to manage emergencies, offer normal treatment, and meet the demands of guests.

1. Mountain Rescue Service (Air Zermatt)
Address:: Heliport, 3920 Zermatt, Switzerland

Air Zermatt is a well-known alpine rescue service that serves the Zermatt region. Given the hard terrain and popularity of high-altitude sports, Air Zermatt is critical to guarantee the safety of hikers, climbers, and skiers.

Services
- **Rescue Operations:** Helicopter rescues for those in trouble or wounded in distant and difficult-to-access regions.
- **Medical Transport:** If you have a major injury or an emergency, Air Zermatt can get you to the hospital quickly.
- **Evacuations:** Emergency services in the event of severe weather or other dangerous situations.
- **Search and Rescue:** Coordinating and carrying out search and rescue activities for missing individuals.

Air Zermatt is noted for its swift reaction times, reaching out to concerned persons within minutes. They work around the clock and have extensive expertise in high-altitude and complex rescues.

2. Pharmacy in Zermatt

Zermatt provides pharmacies for tourists and inhabitants, offering pharmaceuticals, medical supplies, and health advice.

- **Apotheke Zermatt (Address: Bahnhofstrasse 5, 3920 Zermatt, Switzerland)**

Apotheke Zermatt provides prescription and over-the-counter pharmaceuticals, first aid supplies, and health items.

Services

- **Medication Dispensing:** Medication dispensing for both prescription and non-prescription drugs.
- **Health Advice:** Pharmacists provide advice on minor health conditions and might prescribe over-the-counter medications.
- **First Aid Materials:** First aid materials, such as bandages, antiseptics, and pain medications, are essential for treating minor injuries and illnesses.
- **Health Goods:** A wide range of health and wellness goods, including vitamins, supplements, and skincare items.

Pharmacies often open during normal business hours, with some giving longer hours during busy seasons. Emergency pharmaceutical services may be offered outside of usual business hours.

3. Hospitals Near Zermatt

Patients with more acute medical illnesses or who need expert treatment may be sent to bigger hospitals outside of Zermatt. The closest large hospitals are in Visp and Sion.

Visp Hospital (Address: Pflanzettastrasse 8, 3930 Visp, Switzerland)
- **Location:** Visp, around 30 kilometers from Zermatt.
- **Medical Services:** Emergency care, surgery, internal medicine, and specialist departments.

Sion Hospital (Address: Av. du Grand-Champsec 80, 1951 Sion, Switzerland)
- **Location:** Sion, around 75 kilometers from Zermatt.
- **Services:** A full-service hospital providing sophisticated medical care, specialty treatments, and a diverse variety of healthcare services.

4. Emergency Contact Information

Emergency Numbers
- **Medical Emergencies:** 144.
- **Mountain Rescue (Air Zermatt):** 1414; +41275707000
- **General Emergency (Police, Fire, and Ambulance):** 112.

What to Do in an Emergency
- **Stay Calm:** In an emergency, be calm and assess the situation to guarantee safety for yourself and others.
- **Call for Help:** Dial the appropriate emergency number and offer specific details about your location and the nature of the issue.

- **First Aid:** Provide basic first aid as needed and feasible while waiting for expert assistance.
- **Follow Directions:** Obey any directions provided by emergency operators or rescue personnel.

5. Health and Safety Guidelines for Hikers

Preparation
- **Know your Limits:** Choose trails according to your fitness level and expertise.
- **Stay Informed:** Before heading out, check the weather forecast and trail conditions.
- **Carry Essentials:** Always carry essentials such as a map, compass, first aid kit, and extra water and food.

On the Trail
- **Stay on Marked Paths:** Follow marked paths to prevent getting lost and conserve the ecosystem.
- **Hydrate and Eat Regularly:** Keep your energy levels up and keep hydrated.
- **Be Aware of Altitude Sickness:** Ascend gently, remain hydrated, and keep an eye out for symptoms such as headaches, nausea, and dizziness.
- **Use Sunscreen:** Wear sunscreen to protect your skin from the sun, even on overcast days.

Incase of Injury
- **Minor Injuries:** For minor injuries such as cuts, blisters, or strains, use your first aid kit.

Serious Injuries: Contact emergency services immediately and offer as much information as possible to responders.

Zermatt is well-equipped to meet its guests' medical requirements, with a modern clinic, good pharmacy services, and a world-class mountain rescue team. By being aware of these amenities and adhering to safety requirements, you may enjoy your hiking journey in Zermatt with confidence. Always be prepared, familiar with emergency procedures, and respectful of the natural environment to guarantee a safe and pleasurable stay in the Swiss Alps.

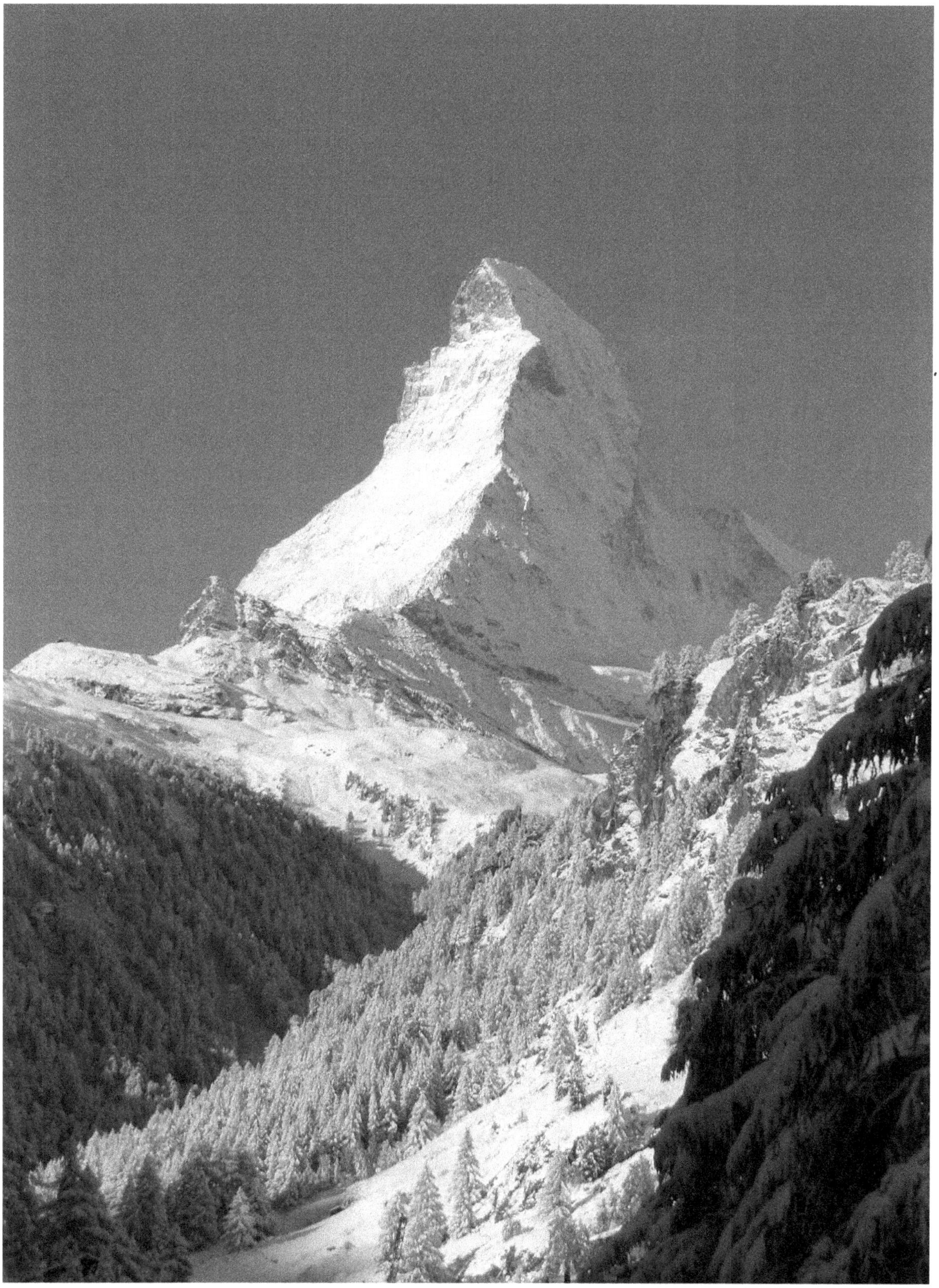

Personal Stories and Testimonials

Zermatt, with its stunning surroundings and renowned Matterhorn, has inspired numerous hikers and explorers over the years. Here, we dig into personal tales and testimonies from people who have hiked its routes, emphasizing their experiences, inspiring trips, and expert advice.

Hikers' Experiences and Stories

1. Emma's First Alpine Adventure
Emma, a new hiker from London, chose to push herself by trekking in Zermatt. She picked the Gornergrat trek because of the panoramic vistas. "Reaching the summit of Gornergrat was a surreal experience," she recalls. "The view of the Matterhorn and its surrounding peaks was worth every step. I had never felt more accomplished or at ease."

2. The Johnson Family's Scenic Walk
The Johnson family, avid hikers from Canada took on the Five Lakes Walk, a family-friendly path with stunning scenery. "It was the perfect hike for us," says Mr. Johnson. "Our children liked identifying various flowers and skipping stones in the lakes. The reflection of the Matterhorn on the beautiful waters was a delight for everyone."

3. Anna and Mark's Romantic Trip to Zmutt
A couple from New York picked this trip for a romantic day out. "The trail to Zmutt was enchanting," Anna recalls. "We strolled through beautiful scenery and lovely Swiss villages. Lunch in Zmutt, surrounded by history and natural beauty, was an amazing experience."

4. David's High-Altitude Challenge
An accomplished hiker from Australia, David attempted the Breithorn climb. "Climbing Breithorn was one of the toughest but most rewarding experiences of my life," he shares. "The high altitude was challenging, but standing at the summit, looking over the vast expanse of snow-covered peaks, was a moment of pure triumph."

Inspirational Hiking Journeys

1. Mia's Solo Journey on the Haute Route
Mia, a seasoned solo hiker from Sweden, took on the multi-day journey from Zermatt to Chamonix. "The Haute Route tested my limits and showed me the true power of

nature," she boasts. "Each day offered new difficulties and breathtaking scenery. The friendship among other hikers and the feeling of accomplishment at the finish made for a wonderful adventure."

2. The Thompson's Tour of Monte Rosa
To commemorate their 10th wedding anniversary, the Thompson couple from the USA organized the Tour of Monte Rosa. "It was an epic adventure," Mrs. Thompson remembers. "We traveled across glaciers, over high mountains, and stayed in wonderful mountain lodges. It was a voyage that enhanced our friendship and provided us with experiences that we will remember forever."

3. Leo's Inspirational Recovery Hike
Leo, an Italian hiker, went to trekking in Zermatt to recuperate from a major illness. "Hiking the Edelweissweg trail was a transformative experience for me," he explains. "Each step seemed like a win, and the beauty of the mountain flowers and scenery raised my spirits. "It reminded me of my inner strength and nature's healing power."

Tips from Experienced Hikers

1. Preparation is the Key: Experienced hikers highlight the need for planning. Always research your trails and check the weather forecast, carry a detailed map, and ensure you have the right gear, especially for high-altitude hikes."

2. Pace Yourself: Don't rush. Take your time, enjoy the scenery, and listen to your body. Hydrate often, and take breaks as required. Hiking is about the journey, not the destination.

3. Respect the Environment: Leave no trace. Respect the paths, animals, and the local communities. Carry out your garbage, stay on indicated trails, and avoid plucking flora or upsetting animals.

4. Embrace Local Culture: Engage with the local culture. Learn a few Swiss German words, sample local cuisine, and see historical landmarks. It enhances your trekking experience and strengthens your connection to the environment.

5. Safety First: Always prioritize safety. Inform someone of your hiking intentions, bring a first-aid kit, and know your emergency contacts. If you have any doubts or are experiencing poor weather, don't be afraid to turn back.

Personal stories and testimonies from hikers in Zermatt demonstrate the transforming influence of trekking in the Swiss Alps. From beginner hikers embarking on their first mountain expedition to seasoned trekkers taking on demanding routes, each journey provides unique insights and inspiration. Seasoned hikers' collective expertise highlights the necessity of planning, pace, environmental stewardship, cultural participation, and safety. These stories and recommendations not only encourage novice hikers to visit Zermatt, but they also provide essential advice for a rewarding and unforgettable hiking trip in this legendary area.

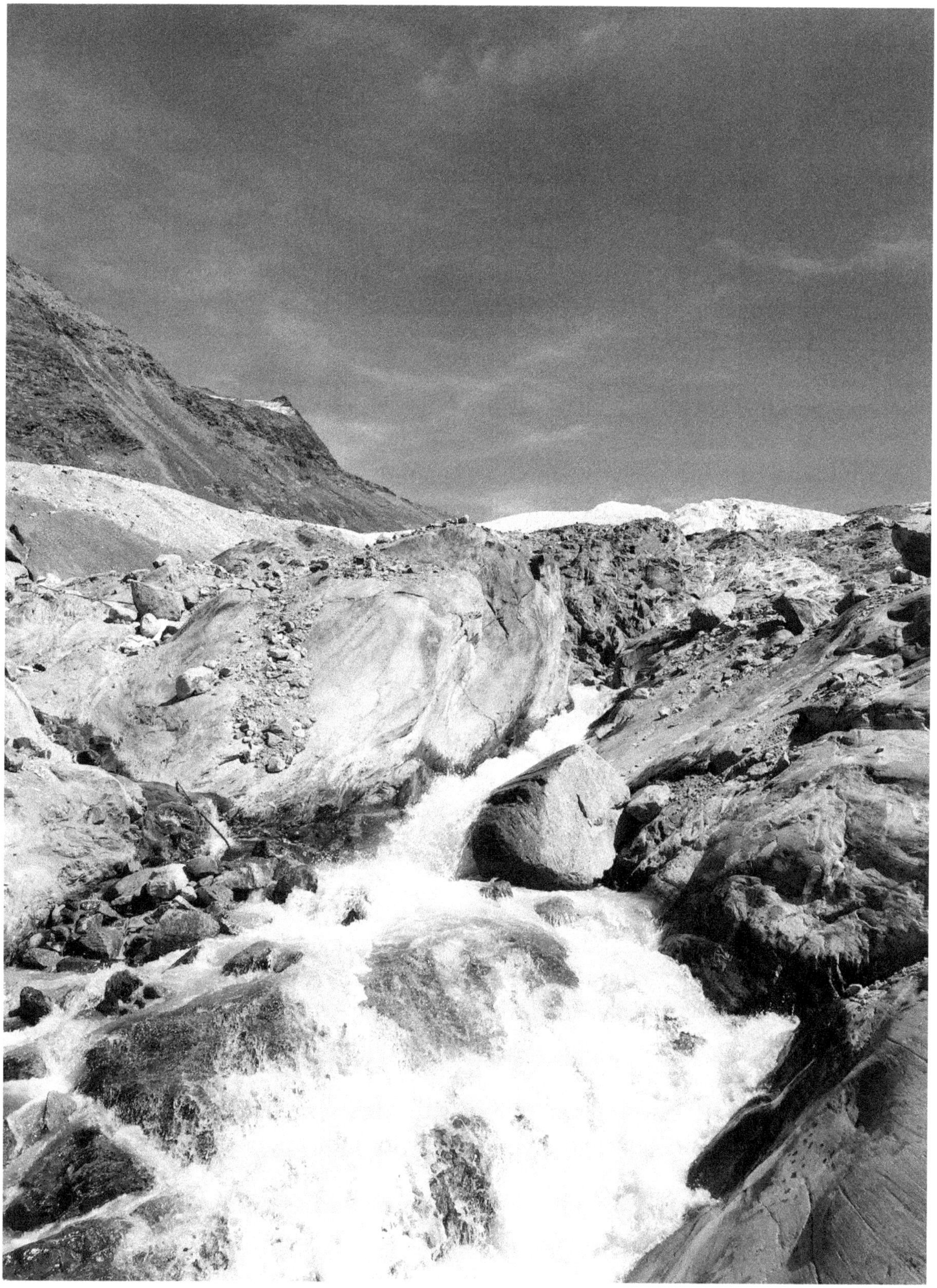

Frequently Asked Questions About Hiking In Zermatt

1. What is the ideal time to hike in Zermatt?

The greatest time to hike in Zermatt is usually from late June to early September. During these months, the weather is typically consistent, and most paths are clear of snow, making for perfect hiking conditions. However, be sure to check local weather predictions since conditions in the Alps may change quickly.

2. Are there any simple paths ideal for beginners and families?

Yes, Zermatt has various family-friendly and beginning paths.
Sunnegga to Findeln: An easy trek with stunning views, ideal for families.
Moos walk: A short, nature-filled walk ideal for youngsters.
Wolli Adventure Park: A family-friendly adventure park with hiking routes.

3. Are there any guided hiking trips offered in Zermatt?

Yes, guided hiking trips are available and highly recommended, particularly on difficult terrain or if you are inexperienced with the region. Guides provide local expertise, safeguard safety, and improve the hiking experience. Local organizations and individual operators provide a variety of trips, from half-day walks to multi-day experiences.

4. What are the safety precautions for trekking in Zermatt?

Stay on Marked Trails: Follow indicated trails to prevent getting lost.
Check weather forecasts: Mountain weather may change rapidly. Always check the forecast and be ready for unexpected developments.
Inform Others: Tell someone about your trekking intentions, including your route and approximate return time.
Altitude Awareness: If you are unfamiliar with high altitudes, do it slowly and give yourself time to acclimate. Stay hydrated and look for indications of altitude sickness.

5. Can I hike to the Matterhorn?

While hiking to the top of the Matterhorn requires sophisticated climbing abilities, various pathways give beautiful views of this renowned peak:
The Matterhorn Trail provides close-up views of the Matterhorn.

Hörnli Hut: A difficult journey to the base camp for Matterhorn climbers that offers an intimate perspective of the peak.

6. What are the most challenging hikes in Zermatt?

For experienced hikers seeking a challenge, Zermatt offers numerous challenging trails:
Hohbalmen: A difficult but rewarding trek with panoramic views.
Breithorn Ascent: This high-altitude expedition requires climbing expertise.
Hörnli Hut: A strenuous walk close to the Matterhorn.

7. Are there any multi-day hiking routes from Zermatt?

Yes, Zermatt is the starting point for numerous famous multi-day treks.
The Haute Route: This traditional trek from Zermatt to Chamonix offers breathtaking mountain vistas.
Monte Rosa Tour: A route that is around the Monte Rosa massif.
Walker's Haute Route: A popular path with diverse scenery and hard sections.

8. How should I physically prepare for trekking in Zermatt?

Aerobic Exercise: To prepare for fitness, engage in aerobic exercises such as jogging, cycling, or swimming to increase endurance.
Strength Training: Squats, lunges, and planks are good exercises for improving leg, core, and back strength.
Hiking Practice: Take local trails to become acclimated to the terrain and height differences. Gradually increase both difficulty and length.

9. What wildlife might I encounter on the trails?

Zermatt's alpine setting supports a variety of wildlife:
Marmots are often sighted along paths, particularly during the warmer months.
Ibex and Chamois: Commonly seen in rocky places.
Birds include eagles, vultures, and alpine choughs.
Flora: Alpine flowers such as edelweiss and gentians bloom abundantly in the summer.

10. Are there any cultural or historical sites on the hiking trails?

Yes, Zermatt's paths often pass past cultural and historical monuments.
Traditional Villages: Discover picturesque Swiss villages complete with rustic cottages and local culture.
Zermatt Museum: Discover the region's rich history and traditions.

Historic Sites: Trails such as the one to Zmutt include historic villages and structures.

11. How can I travel to Zermatt?

Zermatt is accessible by rail and vehicle, despite being a car-free village
By rail: Regular rail services link Zermatt to major Swiss cities. The picturesque Glacier Express is a popular option.
By Car: Drive to Täsch, the closest car-accessible village, and then get a shuttle train or cab to Zermatt.
By Air: The closest major airport is Zurich, which has rail service to Zermatt.

12. What local traditions and etiquette should I be aware of?

Cultural etiquette includes respecting nature and following Leave No Trace principles to safeguard the environment.
Greeting: It is traditional to welcome other hikers with a cheerful "Grüezi" or "Hallo."
Dining: When dining in local restaurants, be mindful of table manners.

Zermatt is a hiker's dream, with a wide variety of paths, magnificent landscapes, and rich cultural experiences. This FAQ section is intended to answer frequent issues and give useful information to help you prepare for your hiking excursion in Zermatt. Your hiking vacation in Zermatt will undoubtedly be memorable and enjoyable if you prepare ahead of time, have adequate gear, and respect the natural and cultural surroundings.

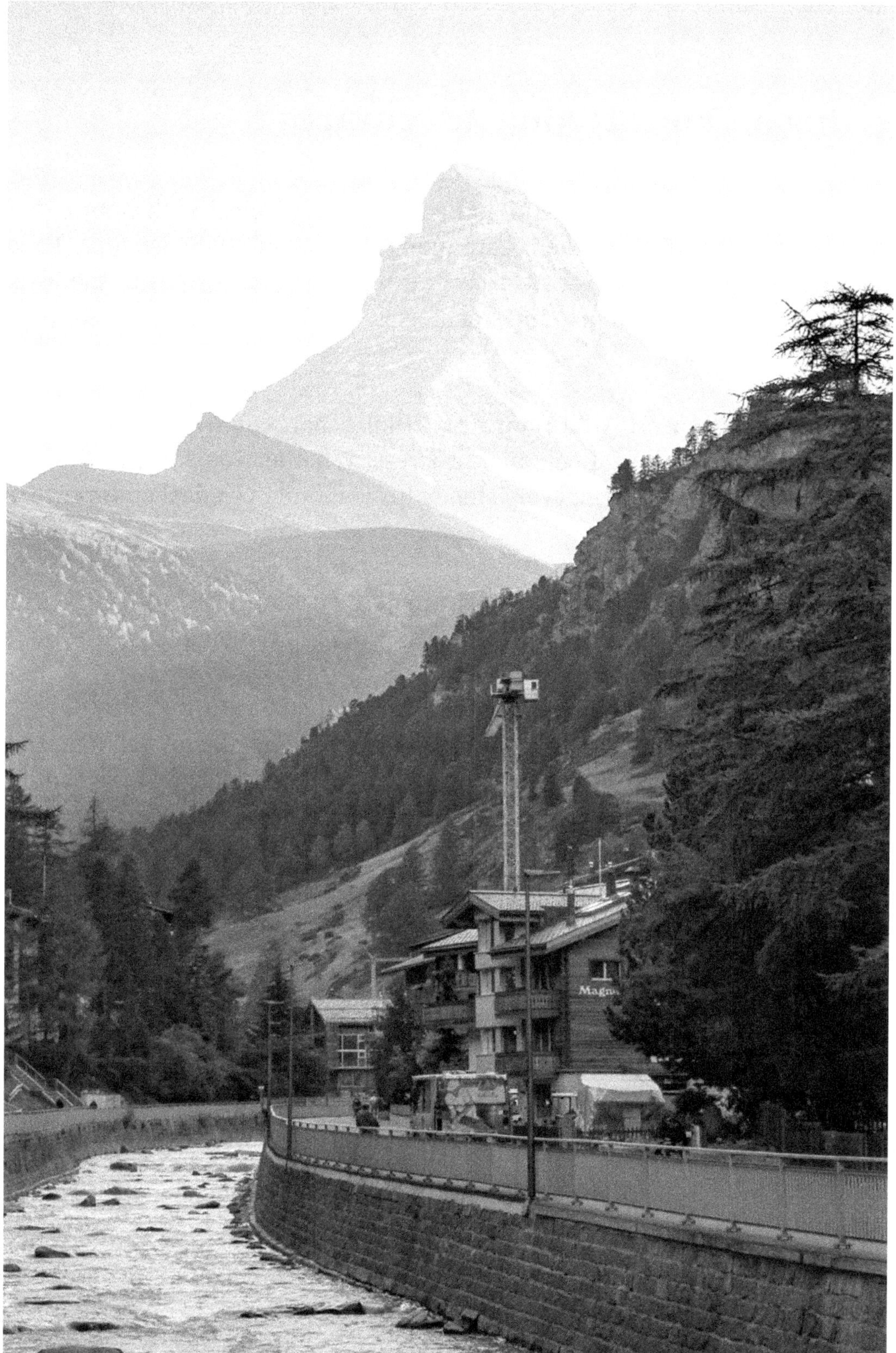

Conclusion

Reflecting on Your Hiking Adventures

Hiking in Zermatt provides an exceptional chance to reconnect with nature, test your limits, and immerse yourself in the breathtaking majesty of the Swiss Alps. Each path, from the magnificent panoramas of Gornergrat to the tranquil lakes of the Five Lakes Walk, offers distinct sensations and memories. When reflecting on your travels, consider the following aspects:

1. Personal Progress and Achievement: Hiking, particularly in hard terrains, may provide a feeling of success and personal progress. Whether you climbed the Breithorn or went for a relaxing family trip, every step helps you build physical endurance, mental resilience, and respect for nature.

2. Nature Connection: Zermatt's paths provide close-up views of the Matterhorn, alpine meadows, and lakes. Consider the moments of amazement and peace you felt, the fauna you saw, and the rare flora you found.

3. Cultural and Historical Insights: Zermatt's paths provide not just natural beauty but also rich history and culture. Your treks, which included typical Swiss communities and historic places along the trails, most certainly provided views into the region's rich legacy. Reflect on the local tales, architecture, and cultural practices that enriched your trip.

4. Shared Experiences: Hiking may build a feeling of friendship. Whether you trekked with friends, and family, or met other travelers along the road, the shared experiences add to the enjoyment of hiking. Consider the companionship, shared obstacles, and common successes that made your walks unforgettable.

Plan Your Next Trip to Zermatt

As you reflect on your previous treks, planning your future trip to Zermatt may be a thrilling task. Consider the following actions to ensure a well-prepared and satisfying return:

1. Exploring New Paths: Zermatt has a diverse network of hiking paths, each with its character. For your next trip, try new paths. Consider pushing yourself with difficult treks like the Hörnli Hut or exploring new picturesque paths like the Edelweiss Weg.

2. Multi-Day Adventures: Plan a multi-day hiking expedition if you haven't done so before. Trails such as the Haute Route and the Tour of Monte Rosa enable a deeper immersion into the alpine scenery while also providing an incomparable feeling of achievement.

3. Seasonal Visits: Zermatt's attractiveness varies with the seasons. If you went hiking in the summer, consider returning in the fall to view the bright autumn leaves or in the spring to see the alpine flowers in full bloom. Each season brings a new viewpoint and distinct experiences.

4. Participate in Local Events: Organize your vacation around hiking events and festivals. Participating in events such as the Zermatt Marathon or the Swiss Mountain Marathon might give you a competitive advantage while also providing an opportunity to meet other hikers.

5. Booking Accommodations and Guides: Optimize your hiking experience by staying near the trails you want to explore. Hiring a local guide may also give useful insights, assure safety, and improve your trekking experience with local expertise.

Final Tips and Advice

As you plan your next hiking trip in Zermatt, keep the following ideas and recommendations in mind to guarantee a safe, pleasurable, and gratifying experience:

1. Be Prepared and Informed
- Always check the weather forecast and trail conditions before heading out.
- Bring necessary supplies, such as maps, a first-aid kit, enough water, and adequate clothes for changing weather situations.

2. Respect Nature and Local Culture
- Follow Leave No Trace principles. Carry out any rubbish, stick to defined pathways, and avoid disturbing animals.
- Respect local norms and participate in the local culture. Learning a few simple words in Swiss German will help you engage more effectively and demonstrate respect for the local population.

3. Prioritize Safety
- Inform someone about your hiking goals and expected return time, particularly if trekking alone.
- Be mindful of altitude sickness symptoms and take appropriate measures, such as gradually acclimatizing and keeping hydrated.
- Know who to call in an emergency and have a strategy in place for unanticipated events.

4. Take Care of Your Health
- Prepare physically for treks. Regular exercise, a good diet, and enough relaxation are essential.
- Pay attention to your body and maintain a healthy pace. Take pauses as required and avoid pushing yourself beyond your capabilities.

5. Embrace the Journey
- Focus on the journey rather than the goal. Enjoy the stunning sights, the sounds of nature, and the feeling of freedom that hiking provides.
- Document your adventures with images or a notebook. Reflecting on these experiences may give long-term delight and inspiration.

Hiking in Zermatt is a unique experience that combines physical difficulty, natural beauty, and cultural diversity. Reflecting on your trips helps you to appreciate the personal development, relationships, and memories you've made. Planning your next vacation opens up new avenues for research and discovery, and following practical guidelines and guidance assures a safe and enjoyable travel. As you continue to explore the Zermatt paths, may each trek offer you new experiences, deeper ties with nature, and unforgettable memories.

Happy Hiking